The Art of
BEADED BEADS

Exploring Design, Color & Technique

The Art of
BEADED BEADS

Exploring Design, Color & Technique

Edited by
Jean Campbell

LARK BOOKS

A Division of Sterling Publishing Co., Inc.

New York / London

Editor
Jean Campbell

Coordinating Editor
Terry Krautwurst

Art Director
Stacey Budge

Cover Designer
Barbara Zaretsky

Photographer
Stewart O'Shields

Illustrator
J'aime Allene

Assistant Editors
Rebecca Guthrie
Nathalie Mornu

Associate Art Director
Shannon Yokeley

Assistant Art Director
Lance Wille

Art Production Assistants
Jeff Hamilton
Lance Wille

Editorial Assistance
Delores Gosnell

Editorial Intern
Sue Stigleman

The Library of Congress has cataloged the hardcover edition as follows:

The art of beaded beads : exploring design, color & technique / edited by Jean Campbell.— 1st ed.
   p. cm.
 Includes index.
 ISBN 1-57990-825-X (hardcover)
 1. Beadwork. I. Campbell, Jean, 1964- II. Title.
TT860.A73 2006
745.58'2—dc22

                                2006007340

10 9 8 7 6 5 4 3 2 1

Published by Lark Books, A Division of
Sterling Publishing Co., Inc.
387 Park Avenue South, New York, N.Y. 10016

First Paperback Edition 2010

Text © 2006, Lark Books, A Division of Sterling Publishing Co., Inc.
Illustrations © 2006, Lark Books, A Division of Sterling Publishing Co., Inc.
Photography © 2006, Lark Books, A Division of Sterling Publishing Co., Inc.;
unless otherwise specified

Distributed in Canada by Sterling Publishing,
c/o Canadian Manda Group, 165 Dufferin Street
Toronto, Ontario, Canada M6K 3H6

Distributed in the United Kingdom by GMC Distribution Services,
Castle Place, 166 High Street, Lewes, East Sussex, England BN7 1XU

Distributed in Australia by Capricorn Link (Australia) Pty Ltd.,
P.O. Box 704, Windsor, NSW 2756 Australia

If you have questions or comments about this book, please contact:
Lark Books
67 Broadway
Asheville, NC 28801
(828) 253-0467

Manufactured in China

ISBN 13: 978-1-57990-825-6 (hardcover) 978-1-60059-588-2 (paperback)

For information about custom editions, special sales, premium and corporate purchases, please contact Sterling Special Sales Department at 800-805-5489 or specialsales@sterlingpub.com.

Contents

Introduction 7

Basics. 9

Materials and Tools 9

Beading Terms
    and Techniques 12

Stitching Terms
    and Techniques 14

The Projects

Crisscross Bead 22

Pumpkin Bead. 24

Lava Lamp Bead 27

Swirly Bead. 30

Blooming Flower Beads 33

Dagger Bead. 38

Crystal Ball Bead 41

Sea Anemone Bead 44

Pomegranate Bead 46

Bubble Wrap Bead 50

Industrial-Strength Bead 52

Piñata Bead. 54

Lucky Coin Bead. 57

Dodecahedron Bead 60

Wonder Wheel Bead 64

Prickly Pear Bead 67

Confetti Bead 70

Tetrahedron Bead. 72

Caged Bead. 75

Kiffa Spools. 78

Can-Can Bead 80

Chinese Lantern Bead 82

Bubble Daisy Spacers. 84

Ram's Horn Shell Bead. 86

Tropical Bouquet Bead. 90

Bird's Nest Bead 93

Warring States Bead 96

Firecracker Beads 100

Tablet Bead 102

Feather Bead. 106

Beading Heart Bead 109

Pom-Pom Bead. 112

Baroque Bead. 114

Double Dutch Bead 118

Puffy Mandala Bead 121

Smocked Bead 124

Crystal Sleeve Bead. 127

Cube Bead. 130

Colorful Drum Beads 134

Twirly Bead 138

Designer Profiles. 140

Index 143

Introduction

THE PAST FIFTEEN YEARS have witnessed an explosion of creativity and ingenuity among bead artists. No longer limited to plainly strung necklaces or petite beaded purses, we've brought the craft up to its rightful place in the art world. We've stormed art galleries, permanent exhibitions, and touring shows with stunning, innovative work: three-dimensional portraits, draping installations, intricate wearable art, grand sculptures, and more, all made with beads. And now, many of us are turning our eyes back to the most basic building blocks of our work: beads. What better tribute to what we love than to create a new bead entirely out of beads?

What is a beaded bead? What does one look like? And, most important, what do you do with it? A flip through this book will give you some quick answers. From a practical standpoint, you'll see that beaded beads, like all beads by definition, have a hole though which to string, stitch, or embellish. From a design perspective, however, you'll see that with beaded beads there are no bounds. Some of the beads featured have a tightly woven look and others are loose and freeform. Some of the projects take only minutes to make, while others require a soft chair and a book on tape to keep you company during what may be hours of beading. Some work well as spacers for other beads on a strung piece of jewelry.

> What better tribute to what we love than to create a new bead entirely out of beads?

Many would make beautiful focal pieces on a necklace. Despite their diversity, one thing is clear: beaded beads can be works of art, created completely out of beads. It's not difficult to envision the beads in these pages displayed in little glass cases on slim wooden pedestals in a gallery.

Beaded beads are wonderful to admire, but they're even more gratifying to make. Because of their small size, you'll most likely find it takes much less time to make a beaded bead than it does to make most other off-loom beading projects. Their bite-size dimensions make it easy to taste-test new techniques; if any frustrations arise—tangles, knots, miscounted beads—you can simply start over without shedding tears. Stitching beaded beads is a wonderful way to brush up on old favorite techniques, too, and to investigate new ways to apply them. Because you aren't investing much time, you're freer to explore color and design in ways you might not with a more time-intensive project. Just think: all those benefits packed into one tiny beaded-bead package!

The 40 fabulous-looking beads featured in *The Art of Beaded Beads* were created by bead artists who, perhaps like you, were looking for something different to make, wear, or display. The designers used many of the off-loom standards—herringbone, ladder, peyote, and square stitch; daisy chain, netting, and right-angle weave. They worked their creations flat, made circles, and built tubes. And all along the way they stretched these beading techniques to their sculptural limits to achieve the exact look they wanted. The result is a spectacular array of beautiful beaded beads that you can make by following the step-by-step instructions. But the designers also left plenty of room for you to put your own stamp on the projects. By simply making changes in bead color, texture, shape, or pattern, you'll be able to call the beaded bead you make your very own.

I hope that as you jump into these projects and gain confidence with the techniques, you'll envision all kinds of variations and think of dozens of uses. When you do, your beaded beads, whether worn or displayed, will speak volumes about you. And, like the beads in this book, they'll also speak clearly to the question "What is a beaded bead?" The answer: almost anything you want it to be.

— Jean Campbell

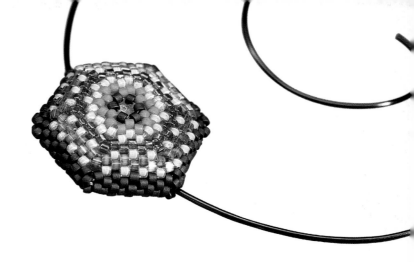

Basics

IF YOU'RE A RELATIVELY new beader, chances are you'll welcome this little tutorial on the basic materials, tools, and techniques needed for creating beaded beads. And if you're a seasoned pro, well, you probably learned a long time ago that a little refresher never hurts!

In either case, keep in mind that this section isn't intended to be a comprehensive primer on beading. Instead, it's designed to serve as a reference to the specific terms and techniques used in this book, so that as you explore the projects you can stitch along without getting tangled up in the instructions.

Let's get started.

MATERIALS AND TOOLS

Choosing the materials for making beaded beads is half of the fun, and much of that fun is choosing the beads themselves. When you shop for the beads you'll use in these projects, the most important thing is to pick colors that please you—after all, you're the one who will be working with those colors. Don't limit your options to just color alone, either. Once you've had some experience making a certain beaded bead and feel confident about your skills, do some experimenting by using differently textured beads or different cuts or shapes.

Choosing the other, perhaps not-so-exciting items on your materials and tools list is important, too. Make sure you're using the strongest thread you're comfortable with, and use the best tools available for the job.

BEADS

There are, of course, hundreds of bead colors, shapes, and types to choose from for making your beaded beads. Here are the main types used in the projects in this book.

Seed Beads

Seed beads, the most common ingredient in the projects featured, are tiny glass beads that range in size from poppy seeds to coriander seeds. The most common sizes are between 6° and 14° (largest to smallest). They come in an enormous range of colors.

Seed beads vary slightly in shape, depending on where they were made. *Czech seed beads* (from the Czech Republic) are somewhat flat, like donuts, and are fairly inconsistent in shape from bead to bead.

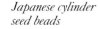
Japanese cylinder seed beads

Japanese seed beads

Czech seed beads

Left to right: wooden bead, bone hair pipe beads, plastic straw

Japanese seed beads have a taller profile than Czech seed beads and are fairly uniform from bead to bead.

Japanese cylinder seed beads have thinner walls than other seed beads and are very uniform in shape. They come in only two sizes—one is comparable to a size 8° seed bead, the other to a size 11°. All the cylinder bead listings in this book refer to the smaller size.

Other Beads

As you look through the project photos, you'll quickly see that seed beads are hardly the only kind used to make beaded beads.

Crystal beads are made from leaded glass and are cut to produce maximum brilliance. The finest of these beads come from Austria. If you are using thread to stitch crystals, buffer them by stringing a seed bead on either side. This helps ensure that the crystal's crisp edges won't cut the thread.

Semiprecious stone beads come in every size and shape imaginable; think of any particular kind of semi-precious stone, and there's bound to be a bead made out of it. The types used in this book (rounds and buttons) are fairly easy to find. Most every stone bead is hewn by hand, and the prices range from pennies apiece on up, depending on the availability, grade, and cut of the stone.

Wooden beads are often used as base beads around which you stitch seed beads. Wooden beads work well as bases because they are generally light in weight and are easily painted. Other base items that work well, too—a bone hair pipe bead (made from a working animal's bone) provides the base for one of the beads in this book, a plastic coffee straw for another, and a simple wooden toy wheel for another.

How Many Seed Beads?

For the instructions in this book, assume that 1 tube of seed beads is sufficient to finish the project. Otherwise, the amount is specified on the materials list.

Cull Your Seed Beads!

Every type of seed bead has at least a slight variance from bead to bead. To produce very even beadwork, you need to *cull* the beads. To do so, carefully go through each bead you intend to work with and place the thinner ones in one pile, the wider ones in another pile, and the average ones in another. If you have a general sense of which beads are thin or thick, you can also do this while you're working, stringing on a thin or a thick bead as needed. Thin beads work well for making increases, and thick ones work well for making decreases.

Crystals (left), Japanese drop beads (middle), semiprecious stone beads (right)

Nylon beading thread is available in a kaleidoscopic spectrum of colors.

Prewaxed nylon beading thread

THREAD

Thread provides the backbone of most beaded beads. Choosing the right one for the job is often as simple as knowing what your options are.

Beading thread is the preferred stitching material used for the projects in this book. It is usually made of nylon, has a silklike feel, is fairly strong, and comes in a wide array of colors. Some beading threads are prewaxed. If the thread you're using isn't, coat it liberally with wax or thread conditioner (see next column).

Monofilament is a tough, fairly durable stringing material developed by the fishing industry. It's available in a clear version that many beaders like, and, because it's stiff enough, you don't need a beading needle to work with it. Knotting can be a challenge, so it's best to use a figure eight knot (page 13).

Braided thread is a fairly supple, very strong, easily knotted synthetic thread that was, like monofilament, developed by the fishing industry. It only comes in white and green, but the thread can be dyed with fabric dyes or colored with permanent markers.

TOOLS

Bead weaving requires no-frills tools, but the few tools necessary are very important. Be sure to use the right tools for the job, or chances are you'll experience serious delays.

Waxes and thread conditioners are used to prepare thread before stitching. These materials help ensure the thread doesn't fray, aid in keeping a firm thread tension, and may even help prevent tangles. The three most used are beeswax, microcrystalline wax, and specially formulated conditioner.

Small, sharp *scissors* are essential for making thread cuts. It's best to have scissors with pointed ends so you can get into tight spots, as well as cut thread close to the work. Embroiderer's scissors work well for this.

Beading needles are very thin needles that can easily pass through seed beads. The most common sizes used are 10, 11, and 12. Beaders primarily use two different types of beading needles: *English beading needles*, which are especially thin and long, and *sharp needles*, which have a stronger body and are somewhat shorter. Both have tiny eyes through which you pass the thread.

Thread conditioner (left), beeswax (right)

Use a *thread burner* or *lighter* to melt the ends of wayward synthetic threads after you trim them. A thread burner is a battery-operated device that was initially intended for wax sculpting. Once warmed up, you simply touch the end of the burner to the thread and the thread melts away. Using a lighter to melt thread ends is not as precise, but it still works. Don't use matches, however—the soot can permanently mar your beadwork.

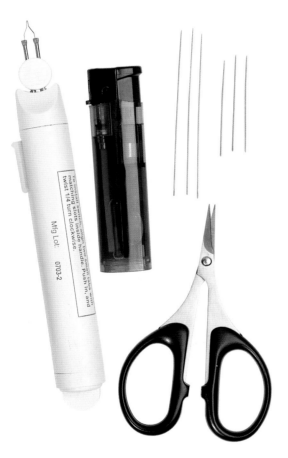

Clockwise from top left: thread burner, lighter, English beading needles, sharp beading needles, embroiderer's scissors

BEADING TERMS AND TECHNIQUES

There are dozens and dozens of beading techniques; the ones listed below are only those necessary to complete the projects in this book.

The project instructions assume you know these techniques inside and out, so please read over this section carefully. Likewise, keep in mind that beading, like almost any endeavor, has its own specialized terminology. You'll have trouble understanding the instructions without at least a passing familiarity with the terms explained in this section.

GENERAL

As you follow the instructions for any one of the projects, you'll likely encounter these general terms and techniques.

A *row* of beadwork is the result of stitching beads in a line back and forth. Multiple rows create a flat piece of beadwork.

A *round* is the result of stitching beads in a circle and then stepping up (page 14). Multiple rounds create circular or tubular pieces of beadwork.

Pass the needle through means you use your needle and thread to go through beads in the same way they were strung. *Pass the needle back through* means you go through the beads in the opposite direction in which they were strung.

Weaving through beads is passing your needle through beads on the body of the beadwork so you can exit elsewhere. When you do this, always keep your thread hidden by passing only through adjacent beads.

Reinforcing the beadwork requires weaving through as many beads as possible on the body of the beadwork. Many beaders like to reinforce the beadwork by passing through beads until the holes are full of thread.

THREAD-RELATED

Many of the terms and techniques you'll run across in the instructions reference thread.

The *tail thread* is the length that remains after you have strung your beads. It is the end farthest away from your needle. The *working thread* is the portion of thread between the needle and the first beads strung. You use it to do your stitching.

To *start a new thread*, pass the thread through the needle and stitch through beads on the body of the beadwork. If desired, tie a knot between beads. Continue to weave through the beads until you exit from the bead where you can keep stitching.

To *end a thread*, make sure you have at least 3 inches (7.5 cm) of thread left and follow the same procedure as for securing thread (page 14).

Thread tension is the degree to which you pull on the thread to tighten the beads into place. Keeping your thread tension consistent is important in beading, especially when making beaded beads. A firm thread tension (pulling tightly on the thread) is required for just about all the projects in this book.

Another way to keep beads in place is to place a *tension* or *stop bead* at the end of the thread before you begin stitching. To add a stop bead,

Know Your Knots

It's important to know how to tie strong knots when working off-loom beadwork. They are necessary for starting up most circular and tubular techniques, and are also helpful when securing thread.

To make a figure eight knot, make a loop with the thread, pass the thread end behind the working thread and in front of the loop, pass the needle through the loop, and pull tight. See figure 1.

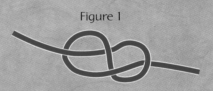

Figure 1

To make an overhand knot, make a loop with the thread, pass the thread end through the loop, and pull tight. See figure 2.

Figure 2

A square knot begins with an overhand knot (above), right end over left end, and finishes with another overhand knot, this time left end over right end. See figure 3.

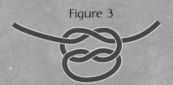

Figure 3

A surgeon's knot is a super-secure form of a square knot (above). You make it the same way, but when you make your first overhand knot, wrap the thread around itself a few times before passing it through the loop. Finish the knot with another overhand knot and pull tight. See figure 4.

Figure 4

string 1 bead and slide it to 1 – 3 inches (2.5 – 7.5 cm) from the end of the thread. Pass through the bead once or twice more. The stop bead will keep any of the beads you add next from slipping off the end of the thread, and is easily removed when necessary.

The most common way to *secure thread* is to weave through several beads on the body of the beadwork (always keeping the thread hidden), tie an overhand knot between beads, pass the needle through several more beads, and pull the thread to hide the knot within the closest bead.

Stretching thread is necessary for certain types of nylon threads because they loosen over time. By stretching the thread between your hands tightly before passing it through the needle, your resulting piece of beadwork will retain its original thread tension.

When you *trim thread*, use the very point of your scissors to get close to the surface of the beadwork. If you pull on the thread slightly and cut, then the trimmed thread will pop back into the beadwork. If you can't trim the thread close enough to the beadwork to hide it, use a thread burner or lighter (page 12) to melt the thread's end. Always be careful not to cut or burn stitched threads.

STITCHING TERMS AND TECHNIQUES

Any type of beadwork in which you are stitching beads together to make a sort of woven beaded fabric is considered bead weaving. Off-loom bead weaving is not done with a loom but only with needle and thread. Following are the terms and techniques related to the off-loom stitches used specifically for the projects in this book. Whenever necessary for completing one or more of the projects, the technique also describes how to make an increase, a decrease, and/or a step up. An *increase* is made when you add more beads than usually used in a stitch. This expands the width or circumference of the beadwork. A *decrease* is made when you use fewer beads than usually used in a stitch. This lessens the width or circumference of the beadwork. When you *step up*, you are positioning your needle in the proper place within the beadwork so you can work another round.

HERRINGBONE STITCH

Herringbone stitch (also known as Ndebele stitch), as its name implies, produces beadwork with a herringbone pattern. The beads in this book use *tubular herringbone stitch* worked off of a ladder-stitched (see next column) foundation round. Exiting up through a bead on the base round, string on 2 beads, then pass the needle down through the next bead on the foundation round and up through the following foundation-round bead. Continue around. Make the last

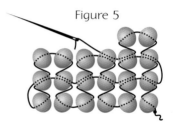

Figure 5

Figure 6

stitch by stringing on 2 beads and passing the needle down into the next bead on the foundation round. *Step up* to the next round by passing up through the first foundation-round bead and the first bead added in this round. String on 2 beads, then pass the needle down through the next bead added in the previous round and up through the next bead. Continue around and step up. See figure 5.

To make a *herringbone stitch increase*, make the 2-bead stitch as usual, pass the needle down through the next bead on the previous round, string on 1 or more beads, and pass the needle up through the next bead on the previous round. See figure 6.

LADDER STITCH

Ladder stitch is often used to make a foundation row for brick or herringbone stitch. To begin, string on 2 beads and pass the needle through them again

Figure 7

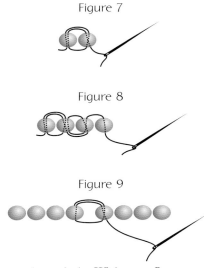

Figure 8

Figure 9

to make a circle. With your fingers, manipulate the beads so they sit side by side. See figure 7.

String on 1 bead and pass the needle down through the second bead initially strung and up through the one just strung. Continue adding 1 bead at a time in this fashion until you reach the desired length. See figure 8. *Note:* If you want your initial ladder row to be more than 1 bead high, start the ladder by stringing on double the amount of beads the row height should be. When you arrange the beads to sit side by side, put them into equal stacks. Each time you make a ladder stitch, string on the amount of beads necessary to make a stack.

To *join the ends* of a ladder-stitched row to make a circle, treat the first bead on the row like a new bead, and stitch them together. See figure 9.

NETTING

Netting creates lacy, open beadwork that looks much like a fishnet. The netting used in this book is *tubular netting* worked off of a foundation circle of beads. After creating the base round, string on an uneven number of beads, skip 1 or more beads on the foundation circle, and pass the needle through the next bead. String on the same number of beads just added. Continue around until you reach the beginning of the foundation circle. *Step up* by weaving the needle through the beads (page 12) to exit from the middle bead added in the first net. String on an uneven number of beads and pass the needle through the middle bead on the next net added in the previous round. Repeat around. When you reach the first net again, pass the needle though the middle bead on the first net of the previous round and the beads on the first net added in this round to exit from the middle bead. See figure 10.

Figure 10

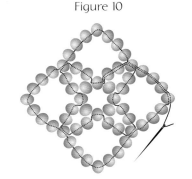

PEYOTE STITCH

Peyote stitch is one of the most popular stitches in contemporary beadwork. Peyote-stitched beads lay in a staggered manner, so the beadwork's surface looks something like a brick wall.

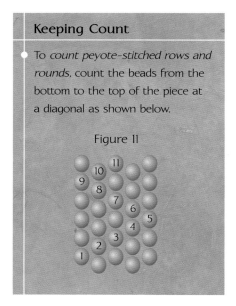
To work *flat, even-count peyote stitch*, string on an even number of beads (this strand will make up your first and second rows). String on 1 bead and pass the needle through the second-to-last bead initially strung. Skip 1 bead and pass the needle through the next bead on the initial strand. Continue across to the end (this completes the third row). Adjust the beads so they look like a spine, and tie a knot with the tail and working thread (page 13) to keep the beads in place. To make the next row, simply string on 1 bead, pass the needle through the last bead added in the previous row, and continue across, adding 1 bead between each bead added in the previous row. See figure 12.

To work *flat, odd-count peyote stitch*, string on an uneven number of beads (this strand will make up your first and second rows). Begin your third row by stringing on 1 bead and passing the

Figure 12

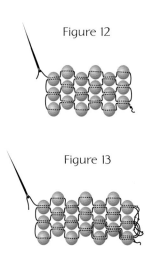

Figure 13

needle through the second-to-last bead initially strung. Skip 1 bead and pass the needle through the next bead on the initial strand. Continue across. When you come to the end of the row, you will end up with 2 beads sitting side by side instead of the tail and working threads exiting from the same bead, as with even-count peyote stitch. So, after you add the last bead, pass the needle through the adjacent bead, and weave through the beads (page 12) to exit from the last bead you added. Work the fourth row in regular peyote stitch. Work the fifth row as you did the third row. You can add the last bead by weaving through the beads in a figure eight, as you did before, or you can simply string on the last bead, pass the needle through the exposed loop of thread between the last two rows, and start the next row. See figure 13.

One-drop peyote stitch is the stitch described above, where you add 1 bead between each bead added in the previous row. To work *two-drop*

peyote stitch, work 2 beads between each bead on the previous round.

Zipping up a piece of flat peyote-stitched beadwork means you'll be connecting it with another piece of beadwork or you'll be connecting the ends of a single piece of beadwork to create a tube. To do so, first make sure that the beads on the rows you're connecting interlock like a zipper (thus the name). If they don't, add or subtract 1 more row to one of the pieces. With the working thread (page 13) exiting from the down bead (see box above) at the end of the last row on the first piece of beadwork, pass the needle through the corresponding up bead (see box above) on the second piece of beadwork. (Or, if making a tube with one piece of beadwork, match the first and last rows together.) Pass the needle through the last up bead on the first piece of beadwork and the corresponding up bead on the second piece. Continue across, lacing the up beads on each piece of beadwork together. The result should look like one continuous piece of beadwork. See figure 14.

Figure 14

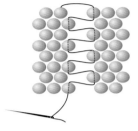

Figure 15

Figure 16

Figure 17

Figure 18

To make a *peyote stitch increase at the end of a row*, add 2 beads instead of 1 to begin the row and continue across. When you come to the increase again, add 1 bead between the 2-bead increase and continue across. Work the following row as you would a regular row. See figure 15.

To make a *peyote stitch increase within a row*, work a stitch with 2 beads instead of the regular 1 bead and continue across. When you work the next row, add 1 bead between the 2-bead increase and continue across. Work the following row as you would a regular row. See figure 16.

To make a *peyote stitch decrease at the end of a row*, don't add that last bead, and then start a new row. It's best to keep your thread hidden for

this decrease either by weaving through beads to set your needle up for the next row or by passing the needle down through the beadwork between adjacent beads, catching the threads there, and passing back up through the beadwork. See figure 17.

To make a *peyote stitch decrease within a row*, pass the needle through 2 up beads on the previous row—without adding a bead—and continue across. When you work the next row, add 1 bead over the decrease and continue across. Work the following row as you would a regular row. See figure 18.

Circular peyote stitch is worked much like flat peyote stitch, but you work in rounds to create a flat circle. Begin by stringing on the specified

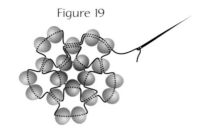

Figure 19

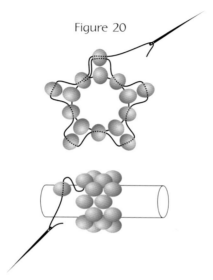

Figure 20

SQUARE STITCH

Square stitch produces a type of bead-work where all the beads sit side by side, creating a grid.

To make *flat square stitch*, string a base strand of beads long enough to make up your first row. String on 1 bead and pass the needle through the last bead strung and the bead just added so the 2 beads sit side by side. String on 1 bead and pass the needle through the next bead on the base strand. Continue across the base strand until you reach the end. Start the next row by stringing on 1 bead and stitching it to the last bead added in the previous row (as you did with the first row). Working in the opposite direction from the first row, continue across, stitching 1 bead to 1 bead. See figures 21 and 22.

Circular square stitch is much like flat square stitch, but you work in rounds to create a flat circle. Begin by stringing on the specified amount of beads. Use a square knot to tie the working and tail threads into a tight foundation circle. String on 1 bead and pass the needle through the bead last exited and the one just strung. Repeat around, stitching 1 bead to 1 bead on the foundation circle. *Step up* to the next round by passing the needle through the first bead added in the round. Working in the opposite direction from the first round, stitch 1 bead to 1 bead all around. As you continue to make rounds, make increases (see next page) as necessary

amount of beads (usually 3 to 5). Use a square knot to tie the working and tail threads (page 13) into a tight foundation circle. Pass the needle through the first bead strung. String on 1 bead, skip 1 bead on the foundation circle, and pass the needle through the next bead. Continue around and *step up* to the next round by passing the needle through the first bead on the foundation circle and the first bead on the current round. *Note:* You step up after each round, passing the needle through the first beads on the previous and current rounds. To widen the circle, you need to work increases between beads every few rounds, always making sure you are adding enough beads so the work doesn't cup. See figure 19.

In *tubular peyote stitch*, you work rounds to create a sculptural tube. Begin by stringing on the specified amount of beads. Use a square knot to tie the beads into a tight circle. Pass the needle through the first bead strung. String on 1 bead, skip 1

bead, and pass the needle through the next bead. Pull tight. Continue around and *step up* to the next round by passing the needle through the first bead on the foundation circle and the first bead on the current round. *Note:* You will step up after each round, passing the needle through the first beads on the previous and current rounds. Repeat, adding 1 bead between each bead on the previous round. Many beaders find it helpful to begin tubular peyote stitch around a form, such as a dowel or a chopstick. See figure 20.

Figure 21

Figure 22

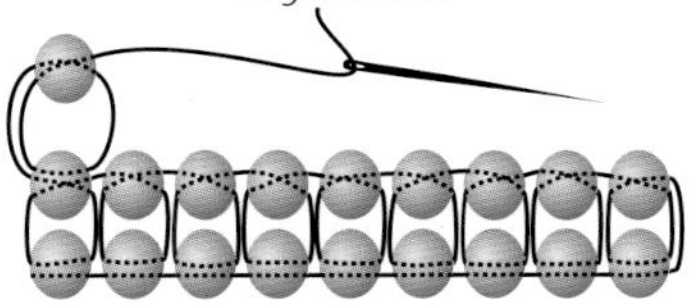

Figure 23

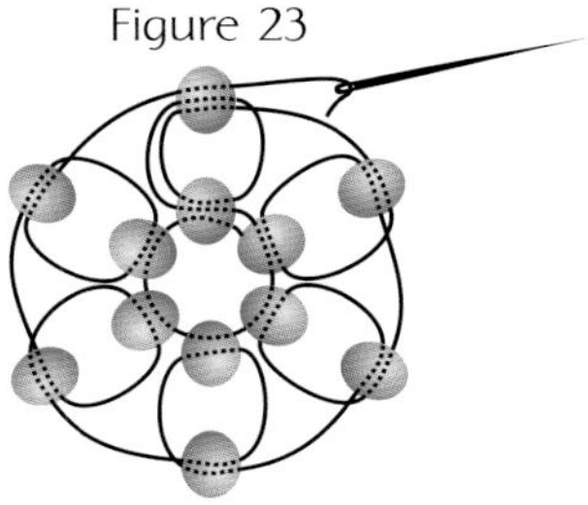

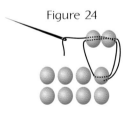

Figure 24

Figure 25

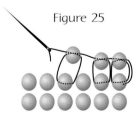

to keep the beadwork from cupping. See figure 23.

Tubular square stitch is done just like circular square stitch, but you don't make increases to keep the work flat. The resulting piece of beadwork is sculptural, shaped like a tube.

To make a *square-stitched increase*, string on more than 1 bead in a stitch. See figure 24.

To make a *square-stitched decrease*, string on 1 bead, skip a bead on the previous row, and stitch it to the following bead. See figure 25.

RIGHT-ANGLE WEAVE

Right-angle weave is a technique that results in square weaves, with each bead (or group of beads) lying at right angles to one another. In this book, each weave is referred to as a *unit*. This technique can be done using either one or two needles.

Begin *flat, single-needle right-angle weave* by stringing on 4 beads. Use a square knot to tie the beads into a tight circle. String on 3 beads and pass the needle through the bead just exited and the first 2 beads just added. Repeat, until you reach the desired row length. See figure 26.

To start the next row, exit up through the first bead positioned along the side of the first row. String on 3 beads and pass the needle up through the side bead just exited, through the 3 beads just strung, and

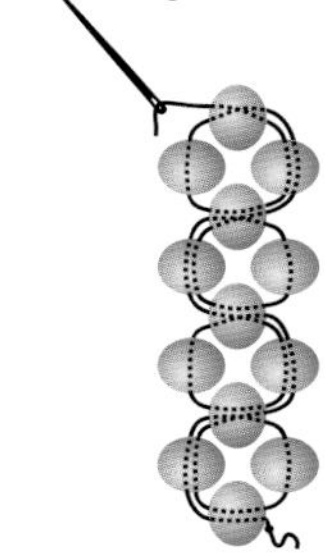

Figure 26

Figure 27

Figure 28

down through the next side bead on the previous row. See figure 27.

String on 2 beads and pass the needle through the third bead added in the previous unit, down through the side bead just exited, and through the first bead just strung. See figure 28.

Figure 29

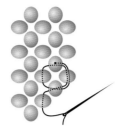

Figure 30

Figure 31

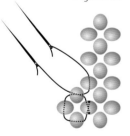

Figure 32

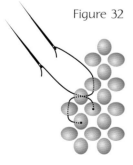

String on 2 beads and pass the needle up through the next side bead on the previous row, through the first bead added in the previous unit, through the 2 beads just strung, and down through the next side bead on the previous row. See figure 29.

Continue working the row this way until you reach the end. Start the new row as you did this one.

Begin *double-needle right angle weave* by threading 1 needle on each end of the thread. String on 4 beads and slide them to the middle of the thread. Pass the needle on your right through the last bead strung. String on 3 beads with the left needle and pass the right needle through the last two beads strung. Repeat, adding 3 beads at a time, until you reach the desired row length. See figure 30.

Turn your work so the first unit of the first row is on top. Weave the needles through the beads so they exit in opposite directions from the first bead positioned along the side of the first row. String on 3 beads with the left needle and pass through the next side bead on the previous row. Pass the right needle through the third bead just strung. See figure 31.

String on 2 beads with the left needle and pass through the next side bead on the previous row. Pass the right needle through the second bead just strung. See figure 32.

Continue working the row this way until you reach the end. Start the new row as you did this one.

To *join the ends* of a right-angle-woven piece of beadwork to make a

Right-Angle Increases and Decreases

 To make a *right-angle-woven increase*, add 1 more bead to a unit and in each of the following rows work an extra unit off of the added bead. See figure 33.

To make a *right-angle-woven decrease*, skip a side bead on the previous row and start the next unit on the following bead. See figure 34.

Figure 33

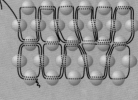

Figure 34

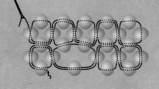

Figure 35
last row   first row

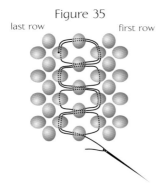

Figure 36

Figure 37

Figure 38

Figure 39

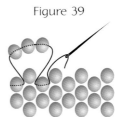

tube, first exit up through a side bead located on the last row in the place where you'd like to make the join. Bend the beadwork so the first and last rows' side beads touch. String on 1 bead and pass the needle down through the corresponding bead in the first row. String on 1 bead and pass the needle up through the side bead last exited on the last row, through the first bead just added, down through the first-row side bead, through the second bead just added, and through the next side bead on the last row.

String on 1 bead and pass the needle up through the next side bead on the first row, through the last bead added, down through the last side bead exited on the last row, through the bead just added, and down through the next side bead on the first row. See figure 35.

Continue working, adding 1 bead at a time and making a figure eight weave, until the rows are joined.

BEADED EMBELLISHMENTS

To make *simple fringe*, string on a length of beads and, skipping the last bead strung, pass the needle back through the rest of the beads just strung. See figure 36.

To make *leaf fringe*, string on 11 beads, skip the last bead strung, and pass the needle back through the second-to-last bead strung. String on 8 beads and pass the needle back through the first bead initially strung. See figure 37.

To make a *picot*, string on 3 beads and pass the needle through a bead adjacent to the one you just exited. See figure 38.

To "*stitch in the ditch*" is to add picots (above) to the body of peyote-stitched beadwork. Start by exiting from a bead where you'd like to add the picot, string on 3 beads, and pass the needle through the next bead on the same row on the body of the beadwork. See figure 39.

Crisscross Bead

This bead's interesting shape makes it a nice spacer for other beads, but it's so unique you'll probably want to make it the featured act. It's constructed by first beading two square-stitched funnels and then stitching the funnels together.

DESIGNED BY
Sharon Bateman

TECHNIQUE
Square stitch

FINISHED SIZE
¾ inch (1.9 cm)

1 With the scissors, cut a 3-foot (91 cm) length of beading thread and pass it through the needle.

2 Work 1 funnel shape using circular square stitch and the following round counts. *Note:* It may help you keep track of your thread path if you remember that each round is worked in the opposite direction from the last one.

ROUND 1: String on 8 A beads and slide them to 4 inches (10.2 cm) from the end of the thread. Use a square knot to tie the beads into a base circle. Pass the needle through the first bead strung.

ROUND 2: String on 2 A beads. Pass the needle back through the next 2 beads on the base circle and through the 2 beads just strung again. Repeat around to add 8 beads in all. Exit from the first 2-bead set added in this round.

ROUND 3: Repeat Round 2 (figure 1) using 8 B beads. *Note:* All the figures show the beads laid out flat for clarity—your beadwork should actually be forming a tube at this point.

ROUND 4: Square stitch a sequence of 2 B beads onto 2 beads and then 3 A beads onto 2 beads twice. You will add 10 beads in all. Exit from the first 2 beads added in this round (figure 2).

ROUND 5: Square stitch 2 B beads onto the 2 beads. On the 3-drop set, stitch 2 C beads onto the first bead, 3 A beads onto the second bead, and 2 C beads onto the third bead. Repeat to complete the round and exit though the first 2 beads (figure 3). You will have added 18 beads in all.

ROUND 6: Square stitch 2 B beads onto the 2-drop bead sets of the last round. On the 3-drop sets, stitch 2 C beads onto the 2 C beads added in the previous round. Stitch 2 D beads onto the first bead of the 3-bead set added in the previous round, 3 A beads onto the second bead, and 2 D beads onto the third bead. Repeat to complete the row and exit though the first 2 beads (figure 4). You will have added 26 beads in all. Secure the thread and trim.

3 Repeat steps 1 and 2 to make another funnel shape. Secure the thread, but don't trim it.

4 Match the 2 funnels with their last rounds touching. Use the working thread of the second funnel to square stitch them together (you won't be adding any beads). Secure the thread and trim. Use the awl to shape the bead as needed.

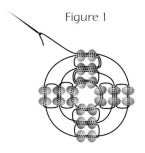

Figure 1

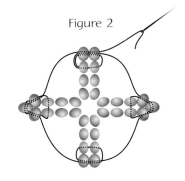

Figure 2

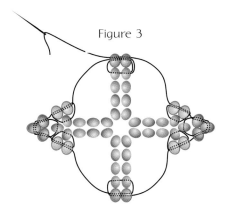

Figure 3

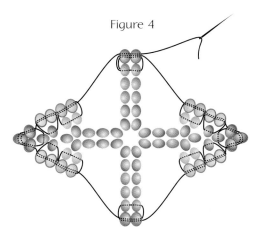

Figure 4

Pumpkin Bead

A challenge for your needle and thread, but a feast for the eyes, these pumpkin-shaped beads look great strung with bold stone or metal beads, on fuzzy fiber, or just solo on a chain. They pair odd-count peyote stitch and different bead sizes to form their telltale wedges.

DESIGNED BY
Marsha Davis

TECHNIQUES
Peyote stitch
Square stitch

FINISHED SIZE
¾ x ⅞ inch
(1.8 x 2.2 cm)

1 With the scissors, cut a 1½-yard (1.4 m) length of beading thread, wax it thoroughly, and pass it through the needle.

2 Make rows of flat odd-count peyote stitch using the following counts (figure 1).

ROWS 1 AND 2: String on 13 D and slide them to 6 inches (15 cm) from the end of the thread.

ROW 3: Work across the row using all D to add 7 beads in all.

ROW 4: Work across the row in the following order: C, C, A, A, C, C.

ROW 5: Work across the row in the following order: C, C, A, A, A, C, C.

ROW 6: Work across the row using A to add 6 beads in all.

ROW 7: Work across the row in the following order: A, A, A, 2 A in one stitch to make an increase, A, A, A.

ROW 8: Work across the row using A to add 6 beads in all. Treat the 2 A on the previous row as 1 bead.

ROW 9: String on 1 A. Square-stitch it to the bead right below it, and then pass the needle through both beads one more time. String on 1 A and pass the needle through the first A just strung on this row (figure 2). This adds the point on one side of the wedge. Work across the rest of the row using A. When you come to the center stitch position, string on 2 A (as in Row 7).

When you reach the end, add another point bead as you did at the beginning of this row.

ROW 10: Work across the row using A to add 6 beads in all. Treat the 2 A on the previous row as 1 bead.

ROW 11: This row begins the decreases and will start to cup the beadwork. Use firm tension and curve the beadwork around your finger to help create the cupping. Work across the row in the following order: C, C, A, A (placed over the 2 A on Row 9), A, C, C.

ROW 12: Work across the row in the following order: C, C, A, A, C, C.

ROW 13: Work across the row using D to add 7 beads in all.

ROW 14: Work across the row using D to add 6 beads in all.

ROW 15: Repeat Row 13.

3 Work Rows 4 through 15 three more times to make 4 connected beaded wedges.

4 Work Rows 4 through 14 once to make a fifth wedge. Secure the tail and working threads and trim.

5 Cut and anchor a new length of thread to the first row created in the first wedge. Work Rows 4 through 13.

6 Zip up the last rows of the fifth and sixth wedges to make a tube. Reinforce the join as needed.

Figure 1

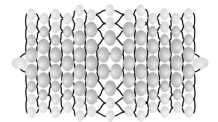

Figure 2

MATERIALS & TOOLS
• Scissors
• Beading thread, size D
• Beeswax
• Beading needle, size 12
• Japanese seed beads in 2 colors (A and B), size 11°
• Japanese seed beads in 2 colors (C, which should match A, and D), size 15°

Among many possible variations: add another seed bead color (far left), squeeze the holes together to make the wedges bulge (left), sew on tiny drops (right), or incorporate crystals into the design (far right).

7 Weave through the beads to exit from one of the point beads. String on 2 C and pass the needle through the point bead on the next wedge. Repeat around to connect all the point beads. Pass the needle through all the beads twice more to reinforce the beadwork. Weave through the beads to exit from a point bead on the other side of the tube, and repeat this step. Secure the thread and trim.

VARIATIONS

Keep the pumpkin bead as is, or gently squeeze the holes together to make the wedges bulge.

Make a permanently flattened pumpkin by working 5 rows of size 15° beads instead of working 3 rows between the wedges. When you sew the point beads together, use 2 size 11° beads between each wedge in place of the 2 size 15° beads. When you squeeze the bead holes together, the beaded bead will remain flat.

Add crystals to the top of the beads. To do so, use a size 15° bead instead of a size 11° bead for the point bead, and then use a 4mm bicone crystal in place of the 2 size 15° beads to connect each point bead.

Use tiny Japanese drop beads in place of the 2 size 15° beads to connect each point bead. Cull the drops to make sure they are all the same thickness. When finished adding the drop beads, help keep them in place by adding another size 15° bead to each side of the drops.

Lava Lamp Bead

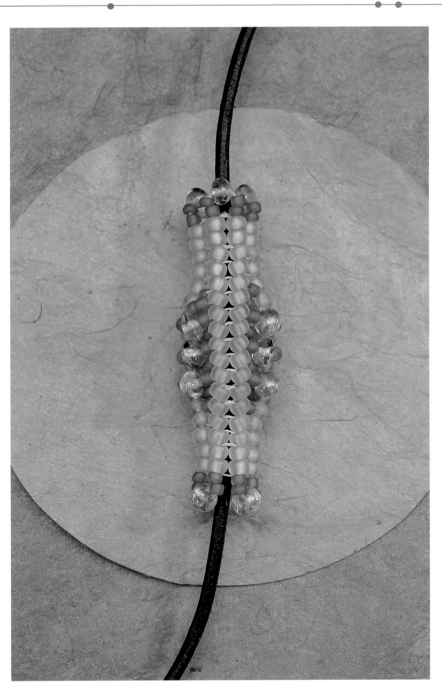

This bead's unique shape draws your eye, but the gems encrusted within it are the real delight. The small semiprecious stones not only beautify this tubular herringbone-stitched bead, but help you make its straightforward increases.

DESIGNED BY
Wendy Ellsworth

TECHNIQUES
Ladder stitch
Herringbone stitch

FINISHED SIZE
**⅝ x 2 inches
(1.6 x 5.1 cm)**

MATERIALS & TOOLS

- Scissors
- Beading thread, size A, to match the size 8° seed beads
- Sharp beading needle, size 12
- Japanese seed beads, size 8°
- Japanese seed beads, size 11°
- 15 semiprecious stone button beads, ⅛ x ³⁄₁₆ inch (3 x 5 mm)

1 With the scissors, cut 11 feet (3.3 m) of thread and pass it through the needle.

2 String on 4 size 8° beads and slide them to 20 inches (50.8 cm) from the end of the thread. Pass the needle through all the beads again to make a circle. Manipulate the beads so they sit side by side in 2 rows of 2 beads each.

3 Make the first 2 rounds of the beaded bead.

ROUNDS 1 AND 2: String on 2 size 8° beads and pass the needle down into the set of 2 beads you just exited and up through the beads just strung. Repeat to make a strip of ladder stitch 6 columns long. Fold the strip so the first and last columns meet. Pass the needle down into the first column added, up through the last

one, and down through the first one again to make a tube.

Note: See figure 1 for bead placement for the entire beaded bead.

4 Make rounds of tubular herring-bone stitch off the ladder-stitched base in the following counts.

ROUND 3: String on 2 size 8° beads and pass the needle down into the next bead on the ladder-stitched base and up through the following bead. Repeat to add 6 size 8° beads in all. Before you pass the needle up through the first bead added in the round to make the step up, double your thread. To do this, pull the loose end down below where it exits the last stitch. Carefully make the step up, trapping the loose end. After a few stitches, the thread will not pull out.

Be sure to make a step up at the end of each of the bead's rounds.

ROUNDS 4 AND 5: String on 2 size 8° beads and pass the needle down through the second bead added in the previous round and up through the third bead. Repeat around to add 6 size 8° beads in all for each round.

ROUND 6: String on 2 size 8° beads and pass the needle down through the second bead added in the previous round. Make an increase by stringing on 1 size 11° bead and passing the needle up through the third bead added in the previous round. Repeat around to add 6 size 8° beads and 3 size 11° beads in all.

ROUND 7: Repeat Round 6 but make the increase by stringing on 2 size

Figure 1

11° beads instead of 1 between the herringbone-stitched columns.

ROUND 8: Repeat Round 6 but make the increase by stringing on 1 size 11° bead, 1 stone button, and 1 size 11° bead.

ROUNDS 9–12: Repeat Rounds 7 and 8. Make sure the increases that include the button beads push to the outside of the beaded tube and the increases that include only size 11° beads go in toward the center of the beaded tube.

ROUND 13: Repeat Round 7.

ROUND 14: Repeat Round 6.

ROUND 15: Repeat Round 5. Secure the thread and trim. Set the beaded tube aside.

Simple fringe in different lengths gives the Lava Lamp Bead a whole new character.

5 Make the final 2 rounds of the beaded tube.

ROUNDS 16 AND 17: Cut a 30-inch (75 cm) length of thread and pass it through the needle. Repeat steps 2 and 3 to make another ladder-stitched tube. Stitch the tube to the last round of the tube already made, weaving your working thread into the beads of Round 15 to mimic a herringbone-stitched thread path. Exit from one of the size 11° beads at the end of the tube that lines up with the place you added your regular herringbone stitches on the body of the tube.

6 String 2 size 11° beads, 1 button, and 2 size 11° beads. Pass the needle down into the next size 8° bead from Round 17 and up through the following size 8° bead. Repeat around to make 3 picots. Secure the thread and trim.

7 Repeat step 6 using the remaining tail thread to add picots to the other side of the beaded tube. Secure the thread and trim.

VARIATION

Add legs of fringe off opposite columns on the herringbone-stitched beads.

Kelly Buntin Johnson
Beaded Face Bead, 1992
40 x 17 x 17 cm
Seed beads, canvas sphere stuffed with cotton batting, wooden dowel, feather; bead embroidery, sewing
Photo © E. G. Schempf

Julie Anick Harper
Hematite Melons, 2006
2 x 2.5 x 2.5 cm
Seed beads, Czech crystals, round hematite beads; tubular right-angle weave, lattice weave embellishment
Photo © Chris Kitchen

Swirly Bead

This seemingly straightforward beaded bead spins with excitement once the patterning comes into play. It's made with right-angle weave over a wooden bead base.

DESIGNED BY
Marcia Laging Cummings

TECHNIQUE
Right-angle weave

FINISHED SIZE
$^{13}/_{16}$ inch (2 cm)

Figure 1

1 Use the permanent marker to color the wooden bead. Set aside.

2 With the scissors, cut a 5-foot (1.5 m) length of thread and pass it through one of the needles.

3 String on 4 B beads and slide them 16 inches (40 cm) from the end of the thread. Pass the needle through all the beads again to form a tight circle. Work right-angle weave, following figure 1.

The color counts for stringing each unit are as follows.

UNIT 2: 1 B, 2 A

UNIT 3: 3 A

UNIT 4: 1 A, 2 B

UNIT 5: 3 B

UNIT 6: 1 B, 2 A

UNIT 7: 3 A

UNIT 8: 1 A, 2 B

UNIT 9: 3 B

UNIT 10: 1 B, 2 A

UNIT 11: 3 A

UNIT 12: 1 A, 2 B

UNIT 13: 3 B

UNIT 14: 1 B, 2 A

UNIT 15: 3 A

4 Join the first and last units together with 1 B bead on top and 1 A bead on the bottom to form a ring. You should have 4 dark and 4 light stripes with a total of 16 units after joining. Step up by exiting through the A bead on the left. (You will step up after each round.)

5 Work the next round, using the following color counts for each unit.

UNIT 1: 2 B, 1 A

UNIT 2: 2 B

UNIT 3: 2 A

UNIT 4: 2 A

UNIT 5: 2 B

UNIT 6: 2 B

UNIT 7: 2 A

UNIT 8: 2 A

Repeat Units 1 through 7 from step 5, omitting the 1 A bead of Unit 1. Connect the first and last units with 1 A bead. Step up.

6 Work 4 more rounds of right-angle weave following the established pattern of 2 diagonal stripes of A beads and 2 of B beads. There will now be a total of 6 rounds.

MATERIALS & TOOLS

- Permanent marker to match the A seed beads
- 16mm wooden bead
- Scissors
- Beading thread, size D
- 2 beading needles, size 12
- Japanese seed beads in 1 dark and 1 light color (A and B), size 11°
- Industrial-strength double-sided tape (as needed)
- Chopstick or dowel

7 Slide the beadwork over the equator of the wooden bead. If it doesn't fit snugly, add a small piece of double-sided tape to hold the beadwork in place as you work. Wooden beads may vary slightly in size. If it seems to fit too snugly, you may have to force the beadwork over the wooden bead or sand the bead lightly (be sure to recolor the sanded area) to accommodate the beads. If desired, place the wooden bead on the chopstick to help you hold onto the work.

8 You will now make decreases on each of the end rounds. The decreases will look better if you make them on the dark beads (A), because they recede visually. Using the working thread, make 1 decrease on each diagonal A stripe. You should have 4 decreases. Pass the tail thread through

Gallery

the second needle and repeat the decreases on the other side of the bead. Pass 1 of the needles through the top beads of the last round's units 2 or 3 times to tighten them around the hole. Repeat with the other needle on the second half of the bead. Secure the working and tail threads and trim. The finished bead will have 8 rounds, including the 2 decreased ends.

Note: If your final decrease round doesn't come as close to the hole as you'd like, work a round of tubular peyote stitch to reach the hole, and then tighten as described above.

TIP

The bead's swirl can go left or right, depending on your second unit's configuration. The instructions describe a bead whose stripes slant right. If you are making many beads for a piece of jewelry, you may want to make some of each to balance the overall design.

JoAnn Baumann
Piñata Necklace, 2004

61 cm long (necklace). Seed beads, pressed glass beads; Ndebele stitch
Photo © Larry Sanders

Blooming Flower Beads

Create a garden-in-the-round of lovely florals, such as the stunning daisy and poppy beaded beads shown here. By beading repeating pattern blocks around a wooden bead, you can create an almost limitless bouquet of designs.

DESIGNED BY
Elfleda Russell

TECHNIQUES
Peyote stitch
Square stitch

FINISHED SIZE:
1⅛ inches (2.8 cm)

TO MAKE A POPPY BEAD

1 Clamp the wooden bead to a firm surface so the hole is horizontal. Drill a hole through the bead vertically so the holes cross at 90° angles. Remove the bead from the clamp.

2 With the brush, paint the bead, including the holes. Let the paint dry.

3 With the scissors, cut a 1-foot (30.5 cm) length of thread and pass it through the needle.

4 String on the wooden bead and pass the needle through it 5 times. Use the working and tail threads to tie a square knot; then slip it into the bead's hole, and trim. Adjust the 5 vertical threads so they are equidistant around the foundation bead, with none in front of the side holes (figure 1).

5 Cut a 1-yard (.9 m) length of thread and pass it through the needle. Use a square knot to tie the end of the thread at the midpoint of one of the foundation bead's vertical threads.

6 Following the chart (figure 2) for color placement, work the top half of the bead using tubular peyote stitch. If a decrease or a 2-drop occurs at the start of a round, step up through either the 2 beads bracketing the decrease or the 2 beads of the 2-drop, plus the first single bead added in the round, to complete the step up.

Figure 1

Figure 2

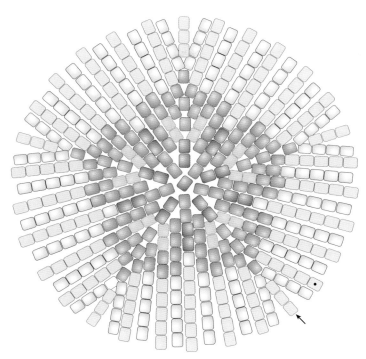

Figure 3

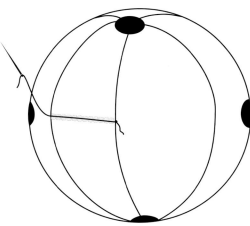

ROUNDS 1 AND 2: Starting at the arrow, string on the first 12 beads, and pass the needle under the next vertical thread on the wooden bead (figure 3). Continue around, always passing under a vertical thread after stringing on 12 beads. Pass through the first bead strung to make the step up. *Note:* Keep in mind that when you string on the beads for Rounds 1 and 2, you are alternating 1 bead from the first round with 1 bead from the second round.

ROUNDS 3–6: Work in normal tubular peyote stitch. For Rounds 3 and 5, pass the needle under the vertical threads as you come to them. This helps hold the beadwork in place.

ROUND 7: Work around, making decreases as shown on the chart. It may help to keep in mind that all decreases are made over the original vertical threads. Pass under the vertical threads as you come to them.

ROUND 8: Work around, adding a 2-drop over each decrease on Round 7.

ROUND 9: Work around, in normal tubular peyote stitch, passing through the 2 beads of each 2-drop on Round 8 as though they are one.

ROUND 10: Work around, adding a single bead above each 2-drop on Round 8.

ROUND 11: Work around in normal tubular peyote stitch.

ROUND 12: Work around, making decreases as shown in the chart.

ROUND 13: Work around, adding a 2-drop above each decrease on Round 12.

ROUND 14: Work around, passing through both beads of the 2-drops added in Round 13.

ROUND 15: Work around, adding 1 bead above each 2-drop added in Round 13.

ROUND 16: Work around in normal tubular peyote stitch.

ROUND 17: Work around, making decreases as shown in the chart.

ROUND 18: Work around, adding 1 bead over the decreases made in Round 17.

ROUND 19: Work around in normal tubular peyote stitch.

ROUND 20: Work around, making decreases as shown in the chart.

ROUND 21: Work around, adding 1 bead over each decrease made in Round 20.

ROUND 22: Following the chart for bead placement, square-stitch 1 bead to each of the up beads added in Round 21. Pass the needle through all 10 beads just added to tighten the round, and then through the 5 red beads to pull them closer to the center.

ROUND 23: Keeping the thread hidden within the beads added in Round 22, stitch the final bead to the center. Secure the thread and trim.

7 Work the second half of the bead. Anchor a new thread so that the first white bead on Round 1 is added in the space marked by the dot in figure 2.

CONNECTING ROUND: Work the entire first round with white beads. When you reach the foundation's side holes, weave the thread through the beads in Rounds 1 and 2 on the first half of the beaded bead to clear the hole and continue around.

ROUNDS 2–5: Repeat Rounds 2 through 5 from the first half of the bead, but when you reach the foundation bead's side holes, work around them as you did on the Connecting Round, always keeping the thread hidden.

ROUNDS 6–23: Repeat Rounds 6 through 23 from the first half of the bead. Secure the threads and trim.

TO MAKE A DAISY BEAD

To make this bead, follow figure 4 and the same general instructions as the Poppy Bead. This design, however, is slightly elongated. Note that the chart has an extra round at the beginning (your first decrease round is Round 8 instead of Round 7). The chart is meant for the first half of the bead, which is completed in 26 rounds. Make the first rounds slightly overlap the top of the foundation bead's side holes. When working the second half of the bead, eliminate Rounds 1, 2, and 3. Start with Round 4, placing its first lavender bead in the space marked by the dot.

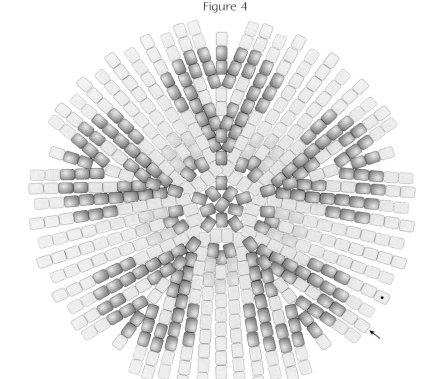

Figure 4

Gallery

Miriam Timmons
Cosmic Beads, 2005
3.8 cm
Seed beads, e-beads, wooden beads;
brick stitch
Photo © artist

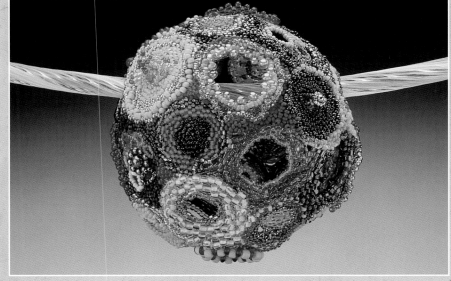

Ann Tevepaugh Mitchell
Meteor Bead: Ode to Joyce, 2006
12 cm
Seed beads, assorted glass beads;
stitched to frame
Photo © Dean Powell

Dagger Bead

These daggers can't hurt you—they're puffy little peyote-stitched beads that dangle beautifully. Make several in graduated lengths and you'll have interesting focal points for a necklace.

DESIGNED BY
Sharon Bateman

TECHNIQUE
Peyote stitch

FINISHED SIZE
$^3/_8$ x $^3/_4$ inch
(0.9 x 1.9 cm)

MATERIALS & TOOLS

- Scissors
- Beading thread, size D
- Beading needle, size 12
- 1 half tube or 1 half hank of seed beads, size 11°

1 With the scissors, cut a 3-foot (91 cm) length of beading thread and pass it through the needle. Put a stop bead at the end of the thread, leaving a 4-inch (10.2 cm) tail.

2 String on the number of beads needed for the desired dagger size (small: 18 beads; medium: 28 beads; large: 38 beads) and let them slide to the stop bead. Pass the needle back through the fourth-to-last bead just strung.

Work peyote stitch down the strand of beads to make what resembles a spine. When the thread exits the last bead, undo the stop bead. Make sure the strip lies straight, and then use the working thread and tail to tie a square knot to secure the beads (figure 1).

3 String on 3 beads and pass the needle back through the bead that has the knot nestled in it and the last bead added in step 2 (figure 2).

4 Work peyote stitch across the bottom of the strip. When you reach the end of the row, string on 1 bead and pass the needle through the bead that lies perpendicular to the rest of the beads at the end of the strip. String on 1 bead and pass the needle through the next bead. Work peyote stitch along the top of the strip. To finish the row, string on 1 bead and pass the needle through the perpendicular bead that lies at the beginning of the strip. String on 1 bead and pass the needle through the first bead on the bottom of the strip. String on 1 bead and pass the needle through the next up bead. Pass the needle through the first bead of the row to make a step up to begin your next row (figure 3).

5 Work peyote stitch across the bottom of the strip. When you reach the end, string on 3 beads and pass the needle into the first bead at the top of the strip. Work peyote stitch across (figure 4).

6 Fold the strip in half so the beginning and end meet. String on 1 bead and pass the needle through the second bead added at the end of the strip in step 5. String on 1 bead and pass the needle through the third bead added at the end of the strip in step 5 (figure 5). This makes the bead's tip.

Figure 1

Figure 2

Figure 3

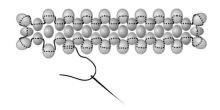

Figure 4

Figure 5

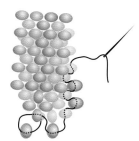

39

7 Continue working peyote stitch down the row until you reach the third up bead from the fold. Weave through the beads so you exit from that up bead, but your needle should point toward the tip (figure 6).

8 Work peyote stitch up to the tip. Pass the needle through the 5 beads of the tip and work the other side of the strip as you did before. Exit from the last bead stitched toward the tip.

9 Zip up one edge of the bead. Weave to the other side and do the same (figure 7).

Figure 6

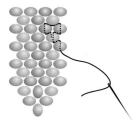

Figure 7

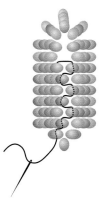

Linda Richmond
Spring Lariat, 2002
2 x 2.5 x 2.5 cm (largest bead)
Cylinder seed beads; peyote stitch
Photo © Dan Richmond

Marissa McConnell
Burst Bead, 2005
3 x 1.5 x 3 cm
Dagger beads, cylinder seed beads, core; peyote stitch, embellishment
Photos © artist

Crystal Ball Bead

This sparkling crystal ball bead can't tell your fortune, but once you finish one, you can bet there will be more in your future. It's made by stitching bicone crystals and cylinder beads together with triangle weave— a cousin to single-needle right-angle weave.

DESIGNED BY
Diane Fitzgerald

TECHNIQUE
Triangle weave

FINISHED SIZE
$7/8$ inch (2.2 cm)

MATERIALS & TOOLS

- Scissors
- Monofilament line, 4-pound (1.8 kg) test
- Sharp needle, size 12
- Thread burner or lighter
- Synthetic or composition wax
- 30 bicone crystals, 5 mm ($^3/_{16}$ inch)
- 60 Japanese cylinder beads

1 With scissors, cut a 3-yard (2.7 m) length of line and pass it through the needle. Bring the ends together and make an overhand knot near the end. Trim the tail close to the knot and melt the ends with a thread burner. Wax the thread thoroughly.

2 String on 1 bicone and 1 cylinder 3 times. Slide the beads 1 inch (2.5 cm) from the knot. Separate the strands between the beads and the knot and pass the needle between the strands. Reverse direction and pass the needle back through the first cylinder and the next bicone (figure 1). Do not allow the knot to slip into a bead.

3 String on 1 cylinder, 1 bicone, 1 cylinder, 1 bicone, and 1 cylinder. Pass the needle through the bicone you last exited and through the first cylinder and bicone just added (figure 2).

4 Repeat step 3 seven more times (figure 3). Lay it out in front of you so that the knot is on the lower left and the needle exits from the outer right bicone. Note that there are 5 bicones sitting horizontally across the top and 4 bicones sitting horizontally across the bottom of the strip. Between these horizontal rows of bicones there are bicones that sit diagonally.

5 Turn the strip into a ring. String on 1 cylinder and pass the needle down through the first diagonal bicone bead at the beginning of the strip. String on 1 cylinder, 1 bicone, and 1 cylinder. Pass the needle up through the bicone your thread just exited at the end of the strip. Pass the needle through the next cylinder to the left and the next bicone to the left (figure 4).

6 Tip the ring so you are looking at it from the top. There should be 5 bicones along the top rim—these are the ring bicones. Make sure your thread is exiting from one of them.

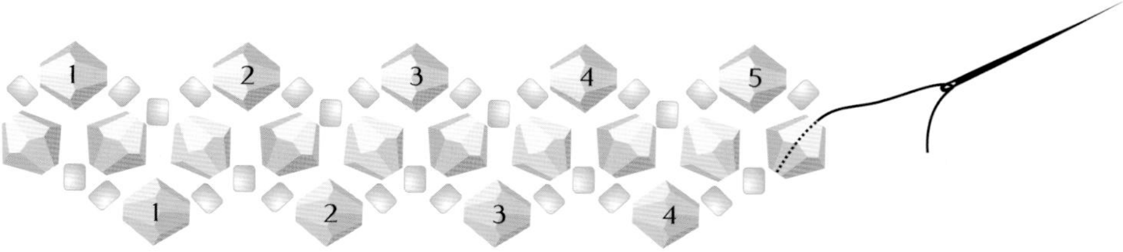

7 Enclose the top of the ball, working clockwise. String on 1 cylinder, 1 bicone, 1 cylinder, 1 bicone, and 1 cylinder. Moving

Figure 3

TIPS

- Take your time. Pass the thread through the beads very slowly to prevent tangling.
- Don't allow the thread to get kinks in it.
- Make sure the thread pulls all the way through the beads and that no loops are formed.
- Keep your thread tension as tight as possible.
- With triangle weave, you should only pass through the bead directly to the right or left of the bead your thread is exiting.

Figure 1

Figure 2

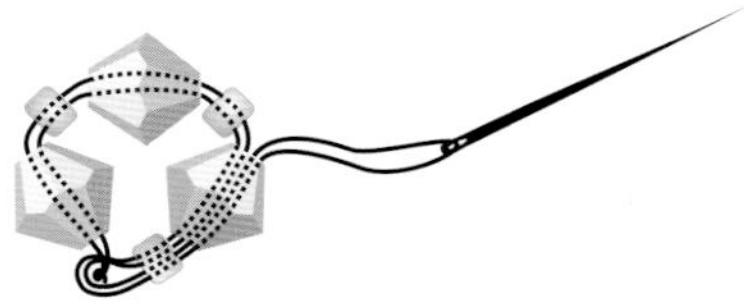

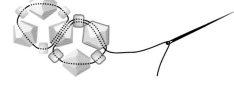

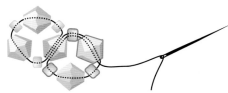

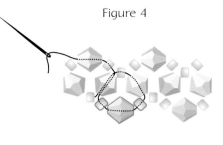

Figure 4

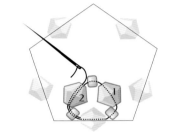

Figure 5

clockwise, pass the needle through the bicone you just exited and the next cylinder and bicone just added (figure 5).

8 String on 1 cylinder, 1 bicone, and 1 cylinder. Pass the needle through the ring's second bicone, going counterclockwise toward the first bicone. String on 1 cylinder and pass the needle through the bicone you just exited and the next cylinder and bicone just added (figure 6).

9 String on 1 cylinder and pass the needle through the next bicone on the ring. String on 1 cylinder, 1 bicone, and 1 cylinder. Pass the needle through the bicone you exited, moving from the center toward the outer ring. Continue through the third bicone in the ring and the next cylinder and bicone (figure 7).

10 String on 1 cylinder, 1 bicone, and 1 cylinder. Pass the needle through the ring's fourth bicone, going toward the previous ring's bicone. String on 1 cylinder and pass the needle through the bicone you just

exited and the next cylinder and bicone just added.

11 Repeat step 9. To complete the top, string on 1 cylinder and pass the needle through the first bicone on the ring, going clockwise. String on 1 cylinder and pass the needle through the first bicone added in the set of 5 for the top. String on 1 cylinder and pass the needle through the fifth bicone on the top and continue through the next cylinder and the next bicone in the ring.

12 Weave to the other side of the ring and complete the other side of the ball by repeating steps 5 through 11.

13 To reinforce the beaded bead, pass the needle through the 5 cylinders at the center of each set of 5 bicones. After reinforcing all the cylinders, pass the needle through the triangles formed by the bicones and cylinders in a random pattern. Work until all the thread is used and the beaded bead is very firm. Trim the thread close to the beads.

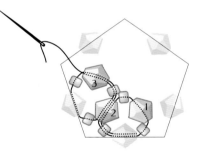

Figure 6

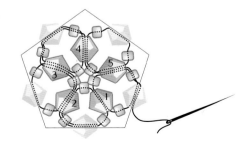

Figure 7

Sea Anemone Bead

These beads might be mistaken for sleeping sea anemones waiting to blossom. They're easy to make with tubular peyote stitch; simply use different seed bead sizes to determine the shaping.

DESIGNED BY
Carole Horn

TECHNIQUE
Peyote stitch

FINISHED SIZE
$\frac{3}{8}$ x $\frac{3}{4}$ inch
(0.9 x 1.9 cm)

1 With the scissors, cut a 1½ yard (1.4 m) length of beading thread and pass it through the needle.

2 Work the first half of the bead as follows.

ROUNDS 1 AND 2: String on 24 size 8° beads and slide them 6 inches (15.2 cm) from the end of the thread. Use a square knot to tie the beads into a base circle. Pass the needle through the first bead strung.

ROUNDS 3–5: Using size 8° beads, work tubular peyote stitch for 3 rounds, making sure you step up after every round.

ROUNDS 6–8: Using size 11° beads, work tubular peyote stitch for 3 rounds.

ROUNDS 9 AND 10: Using size 15° beads, work tubular peyote stitch for 2 rounds.

3 Weave through the beads to exit from an up bead on the first round.

4 Repeat Rounds 6 through 10 in reverse, so that the second half of the bead mirrors the first. Secure the working and tail threads and trim.

MATERIALS & TOOLS

- Scissors
- Beading thread, size D
- Beading needle, size 10
- Japanese seed beads, sizes 8°, 11°, and 15°

Pomegranate Bead

Just like pomegranate seeds, the colorful seed beads in this beaded bead peek out from their little black capsules. You create the bead by mixing right-angle weave, square stitch, and daisy chain; if you have a handle on those stitches, you're good to go.

DESIGNED BY
Sharon Bateman

TECHNIQUES
Right-angle weave
Square stitch
Daisy chain

FINISHED SIZE
**$^3/_8$ x $^3/_{16}$ to 1 inch
(0.9 x 0.4 to 2.5 cm)**

1 With the scissors, cut a 3-foot (91 cm) length of beading thread and pass it through the needle.

2 String on 8 black beads and let them slide 4 inches (10.2 cm) from the end of the thread. Use a square knot to tie the beads into a base circle. Pass the needle through the first bead strung.

3 String on 6 black beads and pass the needle through the 2 beads you last exited and the first 4 beads just strung. Repeat until you've made 5 single-needle right-angle weave units in all. Exit from the sixth bead added in the last unit.

4 String on 6 black beads and pass the needle through the 2 beads you last exited and the first 2 just strung.

String on 4 black beads and pass the needle through the 2 beads at the bottom of Unit 4, through the left side of Unit 6 (the first unit of this row), through the beads just added, and through the bottom of Unit 3 (figure 1). Repeat across the row and exit from the fourth bead added in the last unit.

5 Continue adding rows of right-angle weave until you reach the length you desire (the beaded beads shown are 1 to 7 rows long).

6 Make another layer of beads by square-stitching black seed beads right onto the right-angle-woven strip. Stitch 2 black beads to each vertical bar and 3 black beads to each horizontal bar of the unit. Once you've square-stitched beads to the first right-angle woven unit, string on 1 colorful seed bead. Move across the unit diagonally and pass the needle through the bottom 2 beads of the vertical bar. Pass the needle through the top 2 beads of the same vertical bar (figure 2). If necessary, use the tweezers or pliers to help you maneuver the needle through the beads. The resulting piece of bead-work should look like two layers of right-angle weave. Exit from one of the square-stitched vertical bars.

Figure 1

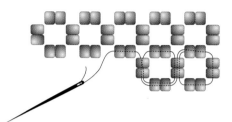

Figure 2

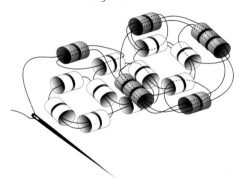

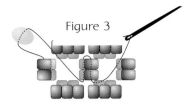

Figure 3

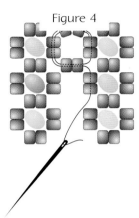

Figure 4

Gallery

7 Repeat step 6, adding 1 colorful seed bead to the center of each unit. Exit from the right-angle weave layer, through the outermost vertical bar of the first unit (figure 3).

8 Finish the bead by rolling the beadwork so the first and last units of the rows meet. String on 2 black seed beads and pass the needle down through the corresponding vertical bar on the last unit. String on 2 black seed beads and pass the needle up through the corresponding vertical bar on the first unit. Pass the needle through all the beads again and down into the first unit on the second row (figure 4).

Continue weaving the ends of the bead together in this fashion. Once you have the right-angle weave layer finished, do the square-stitched one as you did before, adding the colorful center beads.

Linda Richmond
Art Deco, 2002
3 x 2.5 x 2.5 cm (largest bead)
Cylinder seed beads; tubular
peyote stitch
Photos © Dan Richmond

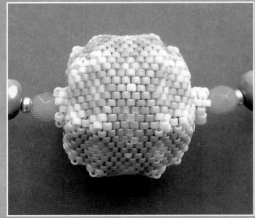

Suzanne Golden
Untitled Group, 2005
25 cm to 45 cm
Plastic beads, glass beads; weaving, fringe,
polyhedron cross-weaving

Bubble Wrap Bead

Bubble wrap beads don't pop when you squeeze them, but making them is just as much fun! You can easily give them a different look by simply changing the bead colors or by creating your own patterns.

DESIGNED BY
Marissa McConnell

TECHNIQUE
Peyote stitch

FINISHED SIZE
$^{1}/_{2}$ x $^{5}/_{8}$ inch (1.2 x 1.5 cm)

1 With the scissors, cut a 1-yard (0.9 cm) length of beading thread, condition it, and pass it through the needle. Put a stop bead at the end of the thread, leaving a 4-inch (10.2 cm) tail.

2 Leaving a 4-inch (10.2 cm) tail, use the seed beads to work a strip of odd-count peyote stitch 9 beads wide and 12 rows long.

3 Bend the strip so the first and last rows touch and the beads interlock. Zip the beads together to create a tube.

4 Weave through the beads so you exit from an end bead with the needle pointing toward the center of the tube (figure 1).

5 String on 1 drop bead and pass the needle through the bead directly across from the one you just exited to "stitch in the ditch"; see figure 2.

6 Repeat step 5 down the tube until you've added 4 drop beads. When you reach the end of the row, pass the needle out through the row's end bead and in through the next end bead on the following row so your needle is pointing toward the center of the tube, as in step 4. Continue adding drop beads as before until you have 6 rows of 4 drop beads each. Secure the thread and trim.

Figure 1

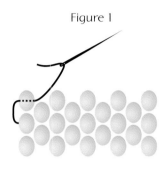

Figure 2

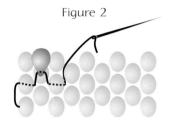

MATERIALS & TOOLS

- Scissors
- Beading thread to match bead color, size D
- Thread conditioner
- Beading needle, size 12
- Japanese seed beads, size 11°
- 24 tiny Japanese drop beads, $\frac{1}{8}$ inch (3 mm)

Industrial-Strength Bead

Who says the only place you can find interesting beads is at a bead shop? This unique, surprisingly beautiful peyote-stitched bead is made with steel nuts from the hardware store.

DESIGNED BY
Ingrid Goldbloom Bloch

TECHNIQUE
Peyote stitch

FINISHED SIZE
**1⅛ x ¾ x ⅝ inch
(2.9 x 1.9 x 1.6 cm)**

MATERIALS & TOOLS

- Scissors
- Heavy-duty waxed beading thread, white
- Permanent marker, metallic silver
- Large beading or small tapestry needle
- 48 size 4 steel hex nuts, ¼ inch (0.6 cm)
- 1 large hex nut, ⅝₆ inch (1.6 cm)

This variation uses a glass bead center and odd-count peyote stitch.

1 With the scissors, cut a 2-yard (1.8 m) length of thread. Press the end of the thread down onto a hard surface with the tip of the marker. Pull the thread through to color it. (*Note:* You can simply buy gray thread, but it won't look as metallic.) Pass the thread through the needle.

2 Work a U-shaped piece of flat even-count peyote stitch, following these row counts.

ROWS 1 AND 2: String on 8 size 4 nuts.

ROWS 3 AND 4: Work across in regular peyote stitch.

ROWS 5–8: Work to make a 2-nut-wide peyote-stitched strip that's connected to Rows 1–4 (figure 1). Weave back through the nuts just added, pass the needle through Row 4, and repeat to make a 2-nut-wide strip as before. Don't cut the working thread. Set aside.

3 Repeat steps 1 and 2.

4 Using the working threads, join the pieces by zipping them up. You'll connect the last nuts on each band to the outside nuts on the first rows (figure 2). Note: Because the pieces are identical, you'll need to turn one of them over so the nuts can interlock.

5 Bend the steel nut frame so it forms a circle. Place the large nut in the center of the steel nut frame. With your fingers, pinch the frame flat to hug the center nut.

6 Secure the working and tail threads and trim.

Figure 1

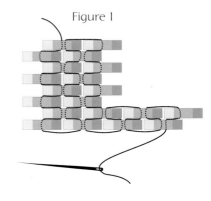

Figure 2

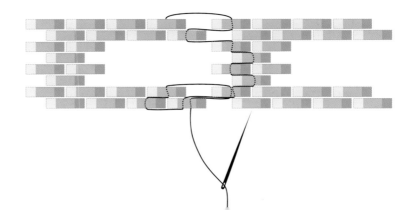

Piñata Bead

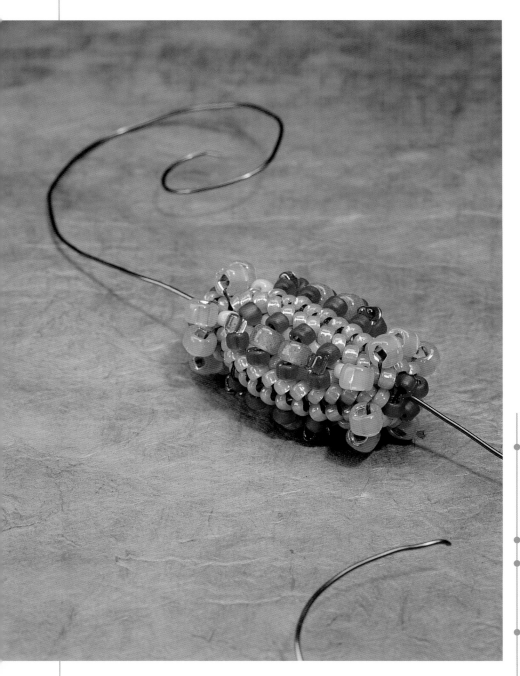

Recipe for a piñata bead: mix seed beads and triangle beads, combine with vibrant colors, and stitch into a cylinder— it's a party! This bead is primarily made using tubular herringbone stitch, but the fiesta really gets going when you make its embellished increases.

DESIGNED BY
JoAnn Baumann and Alyse Middleton

TECHNIQUES
Ladder stitch
Herringbone stitch

FINISHED SIZE
$^{13}/_{16}$ x $1^3/_8$ inches
(2 x 3.5 cm)

TIP

It's important to pull each round very tight, especially when you're making the decreases in Rounds 12–15. Keeping a firm tension will ensure that each of the bead ends is shaped symmetrically.

1 With the scissors, cut a 10-foot (9 m) length of beading thread, double it, and pass it through the needle. Don't wax your thread.

2 Make the base circle (Rounds 1 and 2) using ladder stitch. String on 4 A beads and slide them to 12 to 18 inches (30 to 45 cm) from the thread ends. Pass the needle through all the beads again and pull them tight. Manipulate the beads to make 2 sets of 2 beads sitting side by side. String on 2 A beads. Pass the needle down through the same column of beads you just exited and up through the 2 beads just added. Continue working ladder stitch, using A, until you have a strip 8 beads long. Bend the strip so the first and last columns meet, and ladder-stitch them together.

3 Make the bead's body using herringbone stitch.

ROUND 3: String on 2 A beads and pass the needle down through the top bead on the next column of the base circle and up through the following one. Repeat around the base circle (figure 1). At the end of the round, step up by passing the needle up through the next bead on the base circle and the first bead added in the round. (You'll step up after each round.)

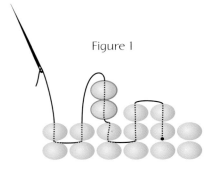

Figure 1

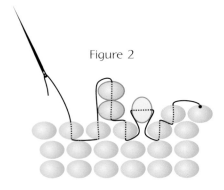

Figure 2

ROUND 4: String on 2 A beads and pass the needle down through the next bead added in the previous round (this column makes up 1 rib). Make an increase by stringing on 1 B bead and passing the needle up through the next bead added in the previous round (figure 2). *Note:* The B bead will stick out slightly from the rest of the beads. Repeat around.

ROUND 5: Repeat Round 4, but use 2 B between the ribs instead of one.

ROUND 6: Repeat Round 4, but use 1 C, 1 triangle, and 1 C between the ribs (figure 3).

ROUND 7: Repeat Round 4, but use 3 B between the ribs. Make sure the previous round's increase pops out, and that this one stays back.

ROUND 8: Repeat Round 4, but use 1 C, 1 lavender size 6°, and 1 C between each rib. Make sure this round pulls forward.

ROUNDS 9 AND 10: Repeat Rounds 7 and 8.

ROUND 11: Repeat Round 7.

ROUND 12: Repeat Round 6.

ROUND 13: Repeat Round 5.

ROUND 14: Repeat Round 4.

ROUNDS 15 AND 16: Repeat Round 3. Exit from the first of the 2 rib beads.

ROUND 17: String on 1 C and pass the needle down through the next bead added in the previous round and up through the following bead. Repeat around (figure 4). Pass the needle through all these beads again to reinforce the work. Exit down through the first bead on one of the ribs.

4 String on 1 orange size 6° bead. Pass the needle up through the next bead on the last round and down through the following bead. Repeat around to add 8 orange size 6° beads in all. They should sit on the outside of Rounds 15 and 16. Secure the thread and trim.

5 Use the tail thread to repeat step 4 on the other end of the bead.

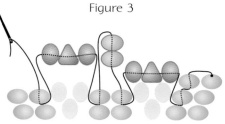

Figure 3

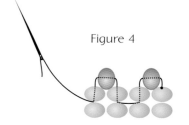

Figure 4

Lucky Coin Bead

Throw a few of these
magical beaded coins
into your jewelry designs
and see what happens!
You'll make them by
connecting two layers of
circular square stitch in
a final round.

DESIGNED BY
Sharon Bateman

TECHNIQUE
Square stitch

FINISHED SIZE
¾ inch (1.9 cm)

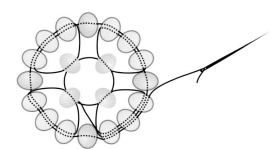

Figure 1

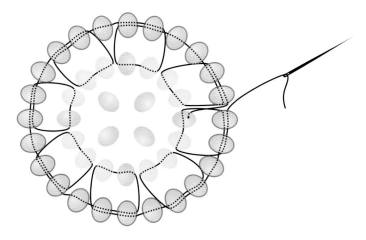

Figure 2

MATERIALS & TOOLS

- Scissors
- Beading thread, size D
- Beading needle, size 12
- Small amount of seed beads in each of 4 colors (A, B, C, D), size 14°

1 With the scissors, cut a 3-foot (91 cm) length of beading thread and pass it through the needle. Work 1 disc using circular square stitch and the following round counts.

ROUND 1: String on 4 A beads and slide them to 4 inches (10.2 cm) from the end of the thread. Use a square knot to tie the beads into a base circle. Pass the needle through the first bead strung.

ROUND 2: String on 3 B beads, then pass the needle through the next bead on the base circle and the 3 beads just strung.

String on 4 B beads, then pass the needle through the next bead on the base circle and the second, third, and fourth beads just strung. Repeat around. String on 1 B bead and pass the needle through the first 3 beads added in this round (figure 1). You will add 16 beads in all.

ROUND 3: String on 2 A beads, then pass the needle through the next 2 beads from Round 2 and the 2 beads just added.

String on 3 A beads, then pass the needle through the next 2 beads from Round 2 and the second and third beads just added. Repeat around. String on 1 A bead, then pass the needle through the first 2 beads added in this round (figure 2). You will add 24 beads in all.

ROUND 4: Repeat Round 3, this time using C beads. You will add 32 beads in all. Exit from the first 2 beads added in this round.

ROUND 5: Repeat Round 3, this time using D beads. You will add 40 beads

in all. Exit from the first 2 beads added in this round.

Secure the thread and trim. Set the disc aside.

2 Repeat step 1, but don't trim the thread.

3 Weave the needle through the beads of the second disc and exit from a bead on Round 3. String on 2 A beads, count 1 bead back from where you exited, then pass the needle through it and 3 more beads from Round 3. Repeat 4 times. Pass the needle through 2 more beads from Round 3.

String on 2 A beads, count 1 bead back from where you exited, then pass the needle through it and 3 more beads from Round 3 (figure 3). Repeat 4 times. This layer will act as a brace between the two discs.

4 Pair the discs so the brace beads from step 3 are in between the two. It will resemble a sandwich cookie with a channel through the "filling" (the channel will make up the bead's

Figure 3

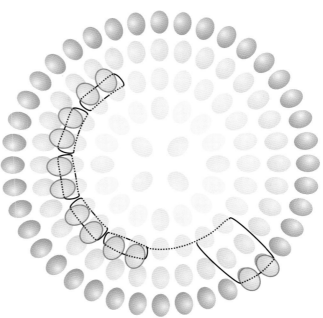

hole). Weave the thread to the edge of the second disc, exiting a bead that lines up with the channel.

5 Work 1 round of 2-bead square stitch around the edge of one disc. String on 2 D beads and pass the needle through the next bead of Round 5, then through the 2 beads just added. Repeat until you've added 18 beads. Pass through 2 more beads of Round 5 (these beads should align with the channel) and continue square-stitching down the other side of the disc. You will add 36 beads in all.

Connect the two discs together by square-stitching the beads you just added in this round to the other disc's Round 5 beads (you won't be adding any beads) (figure 4).

Secure the thread and trim.

Figure 4

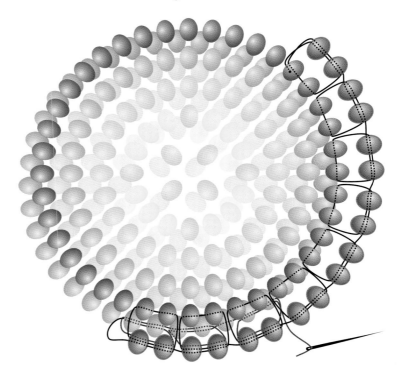

Dodecahedron Bead

It's a bead, it's a box, it's a dodecahedron! This seemingly complex geometric project is really just a matter of constructing 12 simple-to-make beaded pentagons and then joining them to make an edgy sphere.

DESIGNED BY
Diane Fitzgerald

TECHNIQUE
Peyote stitch

FINISHED SIZE
1¼ inches (3.1 cm)

- Scissors
- Beading thread, size D
- Beading needle, size 10
- Synthetic wax
- Thread burner or lighter
- Japanese cylinder beads, 4 grams each in 2 colors (A and B)
- Acrylic floor polish
- Tissues
- Wax paper

1 With the scissors, cut a 1-yard (0.9 m) length of thread and pass it through the needle. Bring the ends together, wax the thread thoroughly so the strands adhere to each other, tie an overhand knot, trim the tail, and melt the ends slightly with a thread burner.

2 Make 1 flat pentagon using circular peyote stitch. Step up at the end of each round. Directions proceed counterclockwise. Work with firm tension. If you are uncertain about recognizing where the step up will occur, count out the number of beads needed for each round. The number of beads needed is shown in parentheses.

ROUND 1: String on 5 A beads and slide them 1 inch (2.5 cm) from the knot. Separate the strands between the beads and the knot and pass the needle between the strands. Tighten so the beads form a base circle. Don't allow the knot to slip into a bead. Reverse direction and pass the needle back through the last bead strung. (5 A)

ROUND 2: String on 1 B bead and pass the needle through the next A bead on the base circle. Repeat 4 more times. Step up by passing the needle through the first bead exited and the first bead added in this round. (5 B) (You will step up after each round.)

ROUND 3: String on 2 A beads and pass the needle through the next B bead on the previous round. Repeat 4 more times (figure 1). (10 A)

ROUND 4: String on 1 A bead and pass the needle through the next A bead added in the previous round. String on 1 B bead and pass the needle through the next A bead added in the previous round. Repeat 4 more times (figure 2). (5 A, 5 B)

ROUND 5: Work the round with B beads. (10 B)

ROUND 6: String on 1 B bead and pass the needle through the next B bead on the previous round. String on 3 A beads and pass the needle through the next B bead on the previous round. Repeat 4 more times. Note on figure 3 that the center bead of the 3 corner beads is indented. Push it in with your fingernail if necessary. (15 A, 5 B)

ROUND 7: String on 1 B bead and pass the needle through the next A bead. *String on 2 A beads and pass the needle through the third A bead on the next set of 3 A beads added in the previous round. Work B beads in the next 2 stitches. Repeat from * 4 more times. (10 A, 10 B)

ROUND 8: String on 1 B bead and pass the needle through the next A bead. *String on 1 A bead and pass

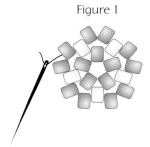

Figure 1

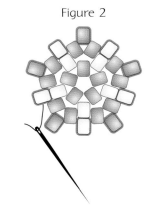

Figure 2

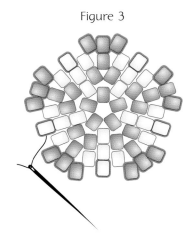

Figure 3

Figure 4

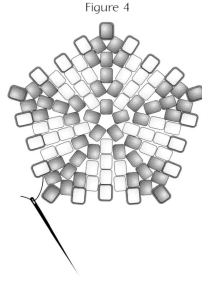

the needle through the next A bead (this adds the corner's point). Work B beads in the next 3 stitches. Repeat from * 4 more times, except on the last repeat work only 2 stitches with B beads (figure 4). (5 A, 15 B)

For a larger pentagon, repeat Rounds 5–8.

Secure the thread and trim.

3 Repeat steps 1 and 2 to make 5 more pentagons. When you make the sixth pentagon, begin with 2 yards (1.8 m) of thread instead of 1 yard (0.9 m), and use B beads to add a ninth round of peyote stitch. Don't trim the thread. This is the base pentagon for the first half of the beaded bead.

4 Use the base pentagon's working thread to join one of its edges to an edge of a second pentagon. Do so by zipping up the beads (figure 5). Repeat to connect one edge of each of the 5 pentagons to the base pentagon. Secure the thread and trim.

5 Anchor a new thread so it exits a corner bead of one of the pentagons (see the arrow in Figure 6). Use B to work peyote stitch counterclockwise along 3 sides of the pentagon. The beads added along the first and second sides are connector beads that will be used to join the second half of the beaded bead to the first half. The beads added to the third side will be zipped together with the side of the next pentagon as shown. Repeat for the remaining pentagons until you have a cup-shaped form. Secure the thread and trim. Set aside.

Figure 5

Base

Figure 6

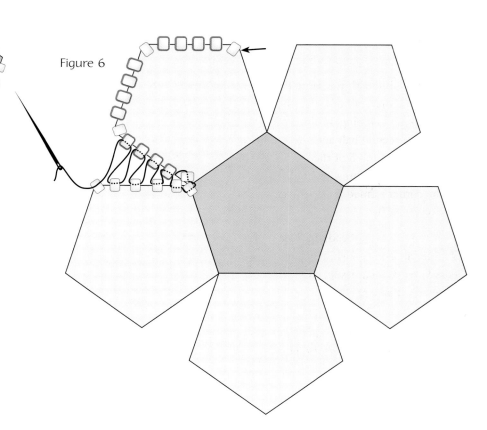

6 Repeat Steps 1–5, joining as described, but add the connector beads only along the edges of each pentagon where they will be joined to form the cup. To do so, weave through beads to the next corner, add the connector beads, and zip up the side.

7 Continuing with the same thread, join the first half of the bead to the second half, zipping up the existing beads in the second half and the row of beads added in Step 5 of the first half. The point of one pentagon should fit into the corner formed by 2 pentagons in the other half.

8 To stiffen the bead, dip it in acrylic floor polish, blot the excess liquid with a tissue, and let it dry on waxed paper.

Diane thanks Julia Pretl and her book, Little Boxes, *for the inspiration for these beads.*

Gallery

Sharri Moroshok
Pearl Sea Anemone Pendant, 2005
5.5 x 3.5 x 3.5 cm
Seed beads, pearls, wooden bead; peyote stitch
Photo © Brian McLernon

Wonder Wheel Bead

An intricate web of sparkling seed beads and tiny teardrops transforms a plain wooden toy wheel into a beautiful beaded bead. You can string this bead horizontally next to other large beads to feature the netted edge, or fashion a beaded bail to show off its pretty face.

DESIGNED BY
Tina Bloomenthal

TECHNIQUES
Peyote stitch
Netting

FINISHED SIZE
**1 x ³⁄₈ inch
(2.5 x 1.2 cm)**

Figure 1

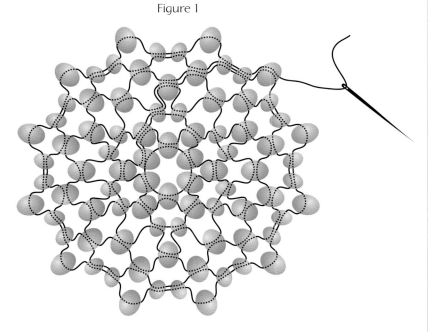

- Wooden wheel/disk (available at craft stores), $^3/_4$ x $^3/_{16}$ inch (19 x 5 mm)
- Fine-grade sandpaper
- Small paintbrush
- Acrylic paint to complement the seed and drop beads
- Scissors
- Beading thread
- 2 beading needles, size 12
- Japanese seed beads, size 11°
- Japanese seed beads, size 15°
- Small amount of industrial-strength double-sided tape
- 36 tiny Japanese drop beads, $^1/_8$ inch (3 mm)

1 Sand the wooden wheel with sandpaper, if necessary. Make sure that the outer edges are smooth because they will be visible through the beadwork. Use the paintbrush to paint the bead. Let the paint dry thoroughly.

2 With the scissors, cut a 5-foot (1.5 m) length of thread and pass it through the needle.

3 Make a beadworked disk using circular peyote stitch. See figure 1 for bead placement.

ROUND 1: String on 6 size 11° beads and slide them down 6 inches (15.2 cm) from the end of the thread. Use a square knot to tie the beads into a base circle. Exit through the first bead strung.

As you work, hold the beadwork firmly between your thumb and forefinger and keep the thread tension light so the beadwork remains flat.

ROUND 2: String on 1 size 11° bead and pass the needle through the next bead added in the base circle. Repeat around to add a total of 6 beads in all. Step up by passing through the first beads added in the last and this round. (You'll step up after each round.)

ROUND 3: String on 2 size 15° beads and pass the needle through the next bead added in the previous round. Repeat around to add 12 beads in all.

ROUND 4: String on 1 size 11° bead and pass the needle through the next bead added in the previous round. Repeat around to add 12 beads in all.

ROUND 5: Repeat Round 4.

ROUND 6: String on 2 size 15° beads and pass the needle through the next bead added in the previous round. Repeat around to add 24 beads in all.

ROUND 7: String on 1 size 11° bead and pass the needle through the next 2 size 15° beads added in the previous round. Repeat around to add 12 beads in all.

Secure the tail thread only and trim. Don't cut the working thread, and leave the needle on the thread. Set aside.

4 Repeat step 3 to make a second beadworked disk.

5 Place a few ⅛-inch (3 mm) pieces of tape around the center hole on each side of the painted wheel. This will help hold the beadwork in place while you complete the bead.

6 Place a beadworked disk on the flat, wide surface on one side of the painted wheel. Place the other disk on the other side of the bead, making sure the Round 7 up beads of each disk are aligned with each other.

7 Use the working thread on one of the disks to string on 3 size 15° beads, 1 drop bead, and 3 size 15° beads. Using firm tension, pass the needle through the next bead added in Round 7. *Note:* The drop bead you add should end up midpoint on the thin side of the painted wheel to make the netting evenly spaced. If your painted wheel is thinner or thicker than the one listed above, you'll need to adjust the bead count of the netting so the drop bead rests in the proper position.

Repeat around to add 84 beads in all (72 size 15° beads, 12 drop beads). Exit from one of the size 11° beads added in this disk's Round 7.

8 Flip the painted wheel over and use the working thread on the second disk to string on 3 size 15° beads. Using firm tension, pass the needle through the corresponding drop bead added in the previous step. String on 3 size 15° beads and pass the needle through the next Round 7 bead. Repeat around to add 72 beads in all. Exit from one of the size 11° beads added in this disk's Round 7.

9 Use the working thread on one of the disks to string on 1 size 15° bead, 1 drop bead, and 1 size 15° bead. Pass the needle through the next bead added in Round 7. Repeat around to add 36 beads in all (24 size 15° beads, 12 drop beads), creating an embellishment along the edge of the painted wheel.

Repeat for the other disk (figure 2).

Figure 2

10 Weave through the netted beads again to reinforce. Secure the thread and trim.

Prickly Pear Bead

Looking a bit like a cactus from a psychedelic desert, this colorful spiraled and fringed bead makes a fun focal point for a necklace, or you can use it as part of a more elaborate design. The technique is a great way to learn spiraled tubular herringbone stitch.

DESIGNED BY
**JoAnn Baumann
and Alyse Middleton**

TECHNIQUES
**Ladder stitch
Herringbone stitch
Fringe**

FINISHED SIZE
**1 x 1⅝ inch
(2.5 x 4.1 cm)**

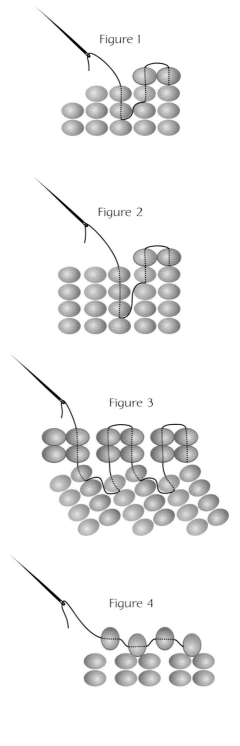

Figure 1

Figure 2

Figure 3

Figure 4

- Scissors
- Prewaxed twisted beading thread
- Beading needle, size 11 or 12
- Japanese seed beads in each of three colors (A, B, C), size 8°
- Japanese seed beads, size 6°

1 With the scissors, cut a 2-yard (1.8 m) length of beading thread and pass it through the needle.

2 String on 4 A beads and let them slide to 18 inches (45 cm) from the end of the thread. Pass the needle through all the beads again to make a circle. With your fingers, manipulate the beads to make two stacks of beads sitting side by side. String on 2 A and pass the needle down through the stack of beads just exited and up through the 2 beads just strung. Repeat to work a strip of ladder stitch 2 beads high and 8 beads long. Join the first and last stacks to make a foundation circle.

3 Work rounds of tubular herringbone stitch off of the foundation circle using the following bead counts.

ROUND 3: String on 1 A and 1 B. Pass the needle down through the next top bead in the foundation circle and up through the following one.

Repeat around to add 8 beads in all. When you come to the end of the round, pass the needle up through first bead added in the previous round and the first bead added in this one to make the step up. (You will make step ups after each round.)

ROUND 4: String on 1 A and 1 B. Using very firm tension, pass the needle down through the next B from Round 3, up through the following A from Round 2, and up through the adjacent A from Round 3 (figure 1). This thread path begins the spiral. Repeat around to add 8 beads in all. At the end of the round you'll step up through 3 beads instead of 2.

ROUNDS 5-17: String on 1 A and 1 B. Pass the needle down through the next B from the previous round, up through the next A from three rounds below, and up through the column to exit from the next A on the previous round (figure 2). Repeat around.

ROUNDS 18 AND 19: At the top of one column, string on 4 A and pass the needle down through the next B in the previous round and up through the following A (figure 3). Repeat around to add 16 beads in all.

4 String on 1 A. Pass the needle down into the next A on the previous round and up through the following A. Repeat around to add 4 beads in all. Exit from the first bead added in this step.

5 String on 1 B and pass the needle through the next A added in step 4 (figure 4). Repeat around to add

4 beads in all. Pull tight to close the top of the beaded bead.

6 Weave through the beads to exit down through a B added in Round 19. String on 1 C, 1 size 6°, and 1 C. Pass the needle back through the size 6° bead. String on 1 C. Skipping the B on the spiral column below the one just exited, pass the needle down through the next B to add a fringe leg to the beaded bead's surface (figure 5). Repeat all the way down the spiral column to add a total of 7 fringe legs.

7 Weave through the beads, skipping the next spiral column of Bs and exiting up through the first B on the following spiral column. Repeat step 6 to add another set of fringe legs. Secure the thread and trim.

8 Pass the tail thread through the needle and repeat steps 4 and 5 to close the other end of the beaded bead. Secure the thread and trim.

Figure 5

Confetti Bead

Celebrate your creative spirit in a big way with these dazzling multicolored beaded beads. Use a single confetti bead as a tassel head or pendant, or string several on a bold necklace.

DESIGNED BY
Nancy Zellers

TECHNIQUE
Right-angle weave

FINISHED SIZE
1 inch (2.5 cm)

MATERIALS & TOOLS

- Permanent markers or paint to match the seed beads
- Base bead, $^3/_4$ inch (2.2 cm), in wood, plastic, resin, or gesso-covered polystyrene foam
- Scissors
- Beading thread to match the base bead color, size B
- Thread conditioner
- Beading needle, size 10 or 12
- Seed beads in a variegated mix, size 11°
- Transparent double-stick tape
- Skewer or toothpick

1 With markers or paint, color the base bead to match the seed beads. Let dry.

2 With the scissors, cut a 1-yard (0.9 m) length of beading thread, condition it, and pass it through the needle.

3 With the seed beads, make a strip of single-needle right-angle weave 3 units wide and long enough to fit around the equator of the base bead. Work the beads in a random color pattern.

4 Place the beadwork around the base bead's equator and weave the strip's first and last units together. *Note:* To keep the beadwork on the base bead, cut a strip of double-stick tape in half lengthwise, place it around the bead's equator, and position the beaded strip over the tape.

5 Weave through the beads so you exit from any of the beads along the edge of the strip. Start a new round of right-angle weave and work around the strip, decreasing as necessary to keep the seed beads flush against the base bead.

6 Continue working rounds of right-angle weave up to the base bead's hole. Each round will probably need 1 or more decreases (the last round usually needs a decrease on every unit).

To finish this half of the bead, pass the needle through the top bead on each of the last round's units. Pull snugly to make a neat ring. Secure the thread and trim.

7 Put a skewer through the bead hole to help keep the beads from sliding around as you work the other half of the bead.

8 Start a new thread on the other side of the bead strip. Cover the second half of the base bead the same way you worked the first half, decreasing as necessary, and ending in a neat ring around the bead hole. Secure the thread and trim.

Tetrahedron Bead

Mathematicians might say that a tetrahedron is a shape with four triangular sides—but as you can plainly see, a tetrahedron can also be sheer beaded-bead beauty! Use a needle to string these hollow beads corner to corner or corner to side.

DESIGNED BY
Diane Fitzgerald

TECHNIQUE
Peyote stitch

FINISHED SIZE
½ inch (1.2 cm)

MATERIALS & TOOLS

- Scissors
- Beading thread, size D
- Beading needle, size 10
- Synthetic wax
- Thread burner or lighter
- Cylinder beads, 4 grams
  each in 2 colors
  (A and B)

Note: You can modify these instructions to make a larger bead than the ½-inch (1.2 cm) one described in these instructions. To do so, simply repeat Round 4 until you reach your desired size, then work Round 5.

1 With the scissors, cut a 1-yard (0.9 m) length of thread, pass it through the needle, bring the ends together, and wax them thoroughly so the strands adhere to each other. Then make an overhand knot, trim the tail, and melt the ends slightly with a thread burner.

2 Using circular peyote stitch and the following round counts, create a triangle.

ROUND 1: String on 3 A beads and slide the beads 1 inch (2.5 cm) from the knot. Separate the strands between the beads and the knot and pass the needle between the strands. Pull tight so the beads form a ring. Don't let the knot slip into a bead. Reverse direction and pass the needle

back through the last bead strung. Pull tight to form a 3-bead triangle.

ROUND 2: * String on 2 A beads and pass the needle through the next A bead on the previous round. Repeat from * 2 more times. Step up by passing the needle through the first bead added in the previous round and the first bead added in this round. (You will step up after each round.) Adjust the beads so the holes in each pair of corner beads are almost parallel.

ROUND 3: * String on 2 A beads and pass the needle into the next A bead on the previous round. String on 1 B bead and pass the needle into the next A bead. Repeat from * 2 more times (figure 1).

ROUND 4: * String on 2 A beads and pass the needle into the next A bead. Work 1 B bead in each of the next 2 stitches. Repeat from * 2 more times.

ROUND 5: Repeat Round 4, but add only 1 A bead at each corner instead of 2 (figure 2). Secure the thread and trim. Set aside.

3 Repeat steps 1 and 2 twice so you have 3 triangles in all.

4 The fourth triangle is made like the first 3 triangles except you begin with a 2-yard (1.8 m) length of thread (prepared as in step 1). Work 1 more round using all B beads (do not add beads at the corners). End by exiting from one of the corner beads.

5 Join 1 triangle to each side of the base triangle by zipping up the edges (figure 3).

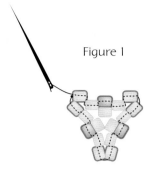

Figure 1

Figure 2

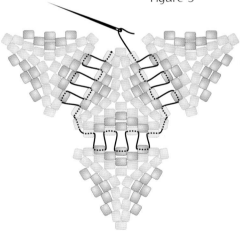

Figure 3

6 Weave through the beads to exit from the outer corner bead of one of the 3 triangles added in the previous step. Work peyote stitch down one side of the triangle. When you reach the corner bead, pass the needle through it, the adjacent corner bead on the base triangle, and then the adjacent corner bead on the next triangle. Pass through all 3 corner beads again to reinforce (figure 4). Fold the 2 adjacent triangles so their outer corners meet and zip them up. Pass the needle through the 3 corner beads again.

7 Repeat step 5 for the remaining sides. Pass the needle through the 3 corner beads again. Secure the thread and trim.

Diane thanks Julia Pretl and her book, Little Boxes, *for the inspiration for these beads.*

Figure 4

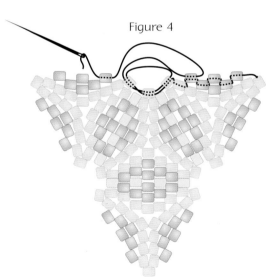

Vary this bead's look by incorporating contrasting beads within the body of each triangle (top) or by making several beads in different sizes and stacking them together (bottom).

Caged Bead

This beaded bead, made by capturing semiprecious stone beads inside a cage of seed beadwork, evokes a double-ended royal scepter. You make the bead by using a flowing combination of herringbone and peyote stitches.

DESIGNED BY
Ruth Ann Grim

TECHNIQUES
Ladder stitch
Herringbone stitch
Peyote stitch

FINISHED SIZE
1¹⁄₂ inches (3.8 cm)

MATERIALS & TOOLS

- Scissors
- Beading thread
- Synthetic wax
- English beading needle, size 10°
- Japanese seed beads, size 8°
- Clear-drying glue or clear nail polish
- Japanese seed beads, size 11°
- 2 round semiprecious stone beads, each ⁹⁄₁₆ inch (1.4 cm)

TIP

When choosing your large beads, make sure that the holes aren't too big—it's easy for the seed beads to slip in—but they should be large enough for several passes of thread.

1 With the scissors, cut a 7-foot (2.1 m) length of beading thread, wax it thoroughly, and pass it through the needle.

2 String on 6 size 8° beads and slide them 6 inches (15.2 cm) from the end of the thread. Use a square knot to tie the beads into a circle. Manipulate the beads so they sit side by side in 2 rows of 3 beads. Add a tiny dab of glue to the knot and let it dry.

3 String on 3 size 8° beads and pass the needle down into the set of 3 beads you just exited and up through the beads just strung. Repeat to make a strip of ladder stitch 8 columns long. Fold the strip so the first and last columns meet. Pass the needle down into the first column added, up through the last one, and down through the first one again to make a tube. Secure the tail thread and trim.

4 Work 3 rounds of tubular herringbone stitch and 1 round of picots, using the following counts.

ROUND 1: String on 2 size 8° beads, and then pass the needle down through the top bead on the next column and up through the following one. Repeat around to add 8 beads in all. Step up by exiting up through the first bead added in the round. (You will step up after every round.)

ROUND 2: String on 2 size 8° beads and pass the needle down through the second bead added in Round 1. Make an increase by stringing on 1 size 11° bead and passing the needle up through the third bead added in Round 1 (figure 1). Repeat around to add 8 size 8° beads and 4 size 11° beads in all.

ROUND 3: Repeat Round 2, but add 2 size 11° beads between herringbone stitches. You will add 8 size 8° beads and 8 size 11° beads in all.

ROUND 4: String on 3 size 11° beads and pass the needle down through the second size 8° beads added in Rounds 3 and 2. Pass the needle through the next 2-bead increase added in

Figure 1

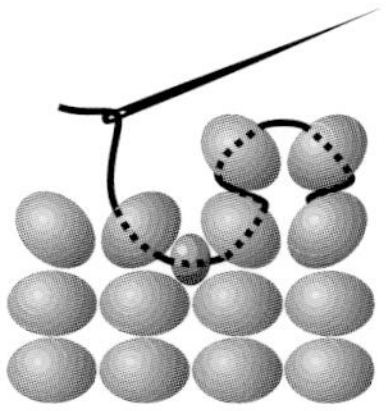

Figure 2

Figure 3

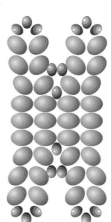

Figure 4

Figure 5

Round 3, and up through the third size 8° beads added in Rounds 2 and 3 (figure 2). Repeat around to add 12 size 11° beads in all. Each set of 3 size 11° beads should make a picot at the top of each herringbone-stitched column.

5 Weave through the beads to exit from a size 8° bead on the other side of the beadwork. The bead you exit should be exactly in line with the last herringbone stitches you made. Repeat step 4 to make the other side of the beaded tube (figure 3). Exit from one of the size 8° beads added in Round 3.

6 String on 7 size 11° beads and 1 stone bead. Pass the needle down through the beaded tube. String on 1 stone bead and 7 size 11° beads. Pass the needle through the 2 size 8° beads that mirror those you just exited and back through the last size 11° bead just strung (figure 4). Make sure

you pass your thread through the bead so that the picot sits on the outside of the strand of size 11° beads.

7 Work flat peyote stitch along the strand of size 11° beads up to the stone bead's hole. Pass the needle through the hole, the beaded tube, the stone bead on the other side of the tube, and the last size 11° bead on the strand added there. Work flat peyote stitch down the strand.

8 Pass the needle down through the herringbone column below the picot, through the adjacent 2-bead increase, and up through the next herringbone column (figure 5). Repeat steps 6 and 7 to create the other 3 peyote-stitched strips to hold the stone bead in place. Flatten the peyote-stitched strips against the stone beads. Secure the thread and trim.

Kiffa Spools

Traditionally, kiffa beads are made by women in remote Mauritanian villages by applying powdered glass to core beads in ancient, finely detailed Islamic patterns. When you make this peyote-stitched version, you can create your own patterns or choose one of the two charted here, including an eye bead, worn as a protective amulet throughout North Africa and many other parts of the world.

DESIGNED BY
Mary Tafoya

TECHNIQUE
Peyote stitch

FINISHED SIZE
$\frac{1}{2}$ x $\frac{7}{16}$ **inch**
(1.3 x 1.1 cm)

MATERIALS & TOOLS

- Small flat paintbrush
- Wooden spool, $\frac{3}{8}$ x $\frac{1}{2}$ inch (1 x 1.3 cm)
- Black acrylic paint
- Scissors
- Beading thread in black, size B or 00
- Beading needle, size 12 or 13
- Small amount of Japanese seed beads, size 15°, in transparent blue AB, opaque black, opaque off-white, opaque canary yellow, and opaque dark red

1 Paint the spool with acrylic paint and let dry completely. Cover with a second coat if desired. For an interesting variation, apply metallic paints or two-part crackle glazes instead of black.

2 With the scissors, cut a 1-yard (0.9 m) length of beading thread and pass it through the needle.

3 Following one of the charts (figure 1), string on the first 2 rows of the pattern. Do so by stringing on the first bead of Row 1, and then stringing on the first bead of Row 2. Continue to alternate rows as you string until you reach the end. Let the beads slide 4 inches (10.2 cm) from the end of the thread, and use a

square knot to tie them in a circle around the spool. Pass the needle through the first bead strung to clear the knot.

4 String on the first bead of the chart's third row, and pass the needle through the next bead in the previous row. Using tubular peyote stitch, continue working around the spool to complete the round. Notice that the first circle of beads shifts to form two rounds. Step up at the end of the round.

5 Follow the pattern to complete all the rounds, stepping up at the end of each round. Weave through the beads to reinforce, secure the thread, and trim.

Figure 1

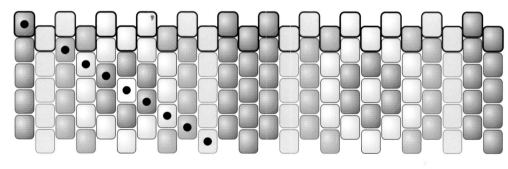

Eye Pattern

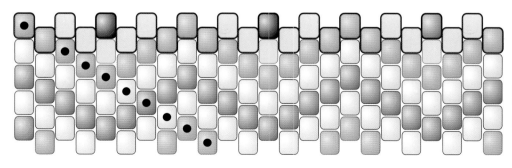

Chevron

Can-Can Bead

Like the ruffled skirts of a Parisian dancer, the spiral that winds down this bead is a vision of motion. The bead is actually two pieces— a peyote-stitched tube and a peyote-stitched spiral—that you make separately and then sew together.

DESIGNED BY
Carole Horn

TECHNIQUE
Peyote stitch

FINISHED SIZE
³⁄₄ x 1 ³⁄₄ inches
(1.9 x 4.4 cm)

MATERIALS & TOOLS

- Scissors
- Beading thread, size D
- Beading needle, size 10
- Japanese seed beads in 3 colors (A, B, and C), size 11°
- Small plastic coffee stirrer, $^3/_{16}$ inch wide x $1^3/_8$ inches long (0.4 x 3.4 cm)

1 With the scissors, cut a 2-yard (1.8 m) length of thread and pass it through the needle.

2 String on 24 A beads and slide them 18 inches (45 cm) from the end of the thread. Work flat even-count peyote stitch for 16 rows.

3 Wrap the beadwork around the coffee stirrer so the first and last rows touch. Zip up the beads to form a tube. If the stirrer is loose in the beaded tube, take one stitch through the plastic and then back into the beadwork. Secure the thread and trim. Set the beaded tube aside.

4 Cut a 1½-yard (1.4 m) length of thread and pass it through the needle.

5 String on 3 B beads and slide them 6 inches (15.2 cm) from the end of the thread. Pass the needle back through the first bead strung toward the tail. Use a square knot to tie the beads into a triangle (figure 1).

6 String on 2 B beads. Pass the needle back through the second bead strung in step 5 and the second one just strung (figure 2).

7 String on 1 B bead. Pass the needle back through the first bead strung in step 6 (figure 3).

At this point, there should be 2 B beads on the end of the beadwork strip you just finished, 1 B bead on the other end, 4 B beads along the top edge, and 2 B beads along the bottom edge.

8 String on 2 B beads and pass the needle through the end bead on the top edge. Without stringing on a new bead, pass the needle back through the second bead of the pair just added. String on 1 B bead and pass the needle back through the first bead of the pair just added (figure 4).

9 Repeat step 8 until the spiral is long enough to wrap around the beaded tube about 3 times. When you are satisfied with the length, secure the spiral's thread and trim.

10 Cut a 2-foot (61 cm) length of thread and pass it through the needle. Anchor the thread to the spiral so it exits from the first bead. String on 3 C beads. Pass the needle under the exposed loop of thread between the next 2 beads on the spiral and up through the third bead just strung.

String on 2 C beads, then pass the needle under the next loop and through the second bead just strung (figure 5). Continue down the spiral until you reach the end.

11 Wrap the ruffle around the beaded tube. Use the tube's tail thread to sew the ruffle into place.

Figure 1

Figure 2

Figure 3

Figure 4

Figure 5

Chinese Lantern Bead

You might find the full-size paper variety of this good-luck design hanging gaily from a boat on the Yangtze River. This miniature glass version begins as a peyote-stitched tube, which you then embellish with loops of beads.

DESIGNED BY
Gillian Lamb

TECHNIQUE
Peyote stitch

FINISHED SIZE
¾ inch (2.2 cm)

1 With the scissors, cut a 4-foot (1.2 m) length of thread and pass it through the needle.

2 Create a beaded tube. String on 14 A beads and work 15 rounds of tubular peyote stitch. Remember to step up after each round. If desired, work around a mandrel or knitting needle to help you keep track of the rounds and maintain consistent tension.

Make a sixteenth round working with B beads. Don't step up. Pull together tightly.

3 Create picot embellishments on the beaded tube's rounds. (The rounds are listed in reverse order to match the way you worked the tube.)

ROUND 15: String on 3 B beads and pass the needle through the next bead on the same round to "stitch in the ditch." Repeat around to add 21 B beads in all (figure 1). Exit from a bead in Round 14.

ROUND 14: String on 3 B beads and stitch in the ditch. Repeat around to add 15 B beads in all. (These beads will be offset from those added in Round 15.) Weave through the beads and exit from a bead in Round 12.

ROUND 12: String on 5 B beads and stitch in the ditch. Repeat around to add 35 B beads in all. Weave through the beads, skip a round, and exit from a bead in Round 10.

ROUND 10: String on 7 B beads and stitch in the ditch. Repeat around to add 49 beads in all. Weave through the beads, skip a round, and exit from a bead in Round 8.

ROUND 8: Repeat Round 10. Exit from a bead in Round 6.

ROUND 6: Repeat Round 10. Exit from a bead in Round 4.

ROUND 4: Repeat Round 12. Exit from a bead in Round 2.

ROUND 2: Repeat Round 14. Exit from a bead in Round 1.

ROUND 1: Work around with B beads. Don't step up. Pull together tightly. Repeat the picot embellishments of Round 15.

4 Secure the thread and trim.

Figure 1

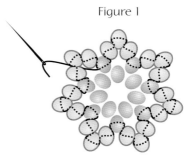

end view

head-on view

MATERIALS & TOOLS

- Scissors
- Beading thread, size D
- Beading needle, size 12
- Japanese seed beads in color A, size 11°
- Mandrel, skewer, or knitting needle (optional)
- Japanese cylinder beads in color B

Bubble Daisy Spacers

You'll change your mind about what daisy spacer beads are after you whip together and use some of these. Color-lined drop beads are especially effective for this project because their inside hue adds a whole new color dimension.

DESIGNED BY
Marissa McConnell

TECHNIQUE
Stringing

FINISHED SIZE
$^5/_{16}$ **inch (0.8 cm)**

MATERIALS & TOOLS

- Scissors
- Beading thread to match bead color, size D
- Beeswax
- Beading needle, size 12
- 5 tiny Japanese drop beads, $\frac{1}{8}$ inch (3 mm)
- Thread burner or lighter

1 With the scissors, cut a 1-foot (30 cm) length of beading thread and wax it thoroughly. Thread the needle and slide it to the middle of the thread.

2 String on 5 drop beads. Use a square knot to tie the working and tail threads together to form the beads into a tight circle.

3 Pass the working thread through the beads several times and remove the needle. Thread the tail with the needle and pass it back through the beads several times. The bead holes should be just about full of thread. Tie an overhand knot between 2 beads, pass the needle through the next bead, and tie another knot. Continue around to secure the circle firmly. Trim and melt the end of the thread with a thread burner.

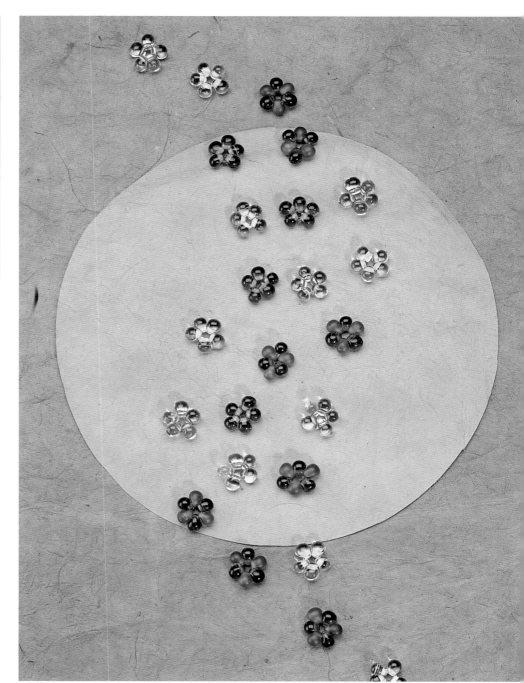

Ram's Horn Shell Bead

You'll evoke seaside dreams when you make this lovely shell look-alike. It's done with sculptural peyote stitch and a sense of adventure—this project is for advanced beaders.

DESIGNED BY
Sharon Bateman

TECHNIQUE
Peyote stitch

FINISHED SIZE
1 inch (2.5 cm) square

Chart

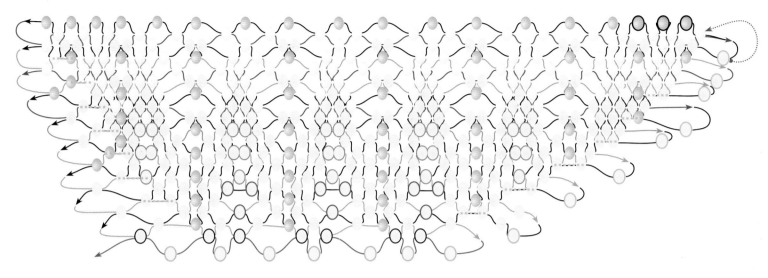

MATERIALS & TOOLS

- Scissors
- Beading thread, size D
- Beading needle, size 12
- Czech seed beads, size 11°, 1 strand each of red-lined amber (A), off-white (B), mauve (C), and peach satin (D)
- Small crochet hook or bamboo skewer
- Awl or darning needle

CHART NOTES

- This chart illustrates bead placement and thread paths for the spirals that begin in step 3 (see next page).

- Begin in the upper corner, indicated by the light green arrow. The thread will be coming out from the last bead of the first spiral. The three beads on top of the base tube are in bold outline.

- The first row of the chart (at top) shows the base tube's red beads.

- The first spiral's beads are at the bottom, outlined in pink.

- The thread path directions are indicated by arrows.

- The lavender dotted lines show thread being passed through beads at the beginning and end of rows.

- The thread paths are shown in different colors for clarity. Red and blue thread paths indicate the rows where there is an increase or decrease. The gray and the black paths indicate regular rows. The green line indicates the place where you zip the spirals together.

- Decreases are outlined in red and blue. The red represents a soft decrease (pass through 2 beads of the previous row; in the next row work 2 beads in one stitch over the decrease; in the following row work 1 bead over the 2 beads). The blue represents a hard decrease (pass through 2 beads of the previous row to make the decrease; in the following row work 1 bead over the decrease).

1 With the scissors, cut a 2-yard (1.8 m) length of thread and pass it through the needle.

2 Using A beads, work tubular peyote stitch to create a tube 12 beads around and 16 rows high. Exit from an up bead on the last round.

3 Make the first spiral.

ROW 1: String on 1 B bead and pass the needle through the next bead from the previous round. Repeat around to create a 15-bead spiral that winds to the bottom of the tube (figure 1). If you like, place the tube on the crochet hook to help you work the rest of the bead.

ROW 2: Weave the needle through the beads to exit back through the last bead added and work peyote stitch up the spiral to add 15 beads in all.

4 Make the second spiral.

ROW 1: Using C beads, work peyote stitch along the top of the tube for 3 stitches and then work a spiral down the tube as you did in step 3 (Figure 2) to add 18 beads in all.

ROW 2: String on 1 C bead and pass the needle through the first up bead. Work 2 D beads (to make an increase). Move up the spiral, working a sequence of 1 C, 2 D in the same stitch (to make an increase) 8 more times to add 27 beads in all.

Note: The 3 C beads added at the top of the tube in Row 1 are part of the second spiral, so be sure to include them as you work the first row.

ROW 3: Pass through the first up bead of the first spiral and through the first D bead of the second spiral. Stitch 1 A bead between the 2 D beads. Work a sequence of 1 C, 1 C, and 1 A between the two D beads of the last row 8 times. End with 1 C bead to add 26 beads in all.

ROW 4: String on 1 C bead and pass the needle through the first 2 up beads on the previous row. Using C beads, peyote-stitch the row for a total of 25 beads.

ROW 5: Pass the needle through the next up bead on the first spiral and the first up bead on the second spiral. Work a sequence of 1 C, 1 C, 2 D (to make an increase) 7 times. End the row with 1 C, 1 C, and 1 A to add 31 beads in all.

ROW 6: String on 1 A bead and pass the needle through the first 2 up beads. Work 1 B, 1 C, and 1 A (on the 2 D beads). Work a sequence of 1 C, 1 B, 1 C, and 1 A (on the 2 D beads) 6 times. End the row with 1 C and 1 B to add 30 beads in all.

ROW 7: Pass the needle through the next up bead on the first spiral and 2 up beads on the second spiral. Work a sequence of 1 C, 1 C, 1 B, and 1 B 7 times to add 28 beads in all.

ROW 8: String on 1 B bead and pass the needle through 2 up beads on the previous row. Work 1 B bead and 1 A bead. Work a sequence of 1 B, 1 C, 1 B, and 2 D (to make an increase) 5 times. End with 1 B, 1 C, 1 B, and 1 A to add 32 beads in all.

Figure 1

Figure 2

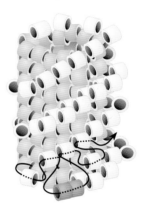

ROW 9: Pass the needle through the next up bead on the first spiral and through the first 2 up beads on the second spiral. Work 1 B, 1 B, 1 B, and 1 A between the 2 D beads on the previous row (to make an increase). Work a sequence of 1 B, 1 B, 1 B, 1 B, and 1 A between the 2 D (to make an increase) 4 times. End with 1 B, 1 B, 1 B, 1 B, 1 B, and 1 B to add 30 beads in all.

ROW 10: String on 1 B bead and pass the needle through the first 2 up beads. Work 1 A and 1 B and pass through the next 2 beads of the previous round (to make a decrease). Work a sequence of 1 B, 1 B, and 1 B, and make a decrease by working 1 B and passing through the next 2 beads of the previous round 5 times. End with 1 B, 1 B, 1 B, 1 B, and 1 B to add 24 beads in all.

ROW 11: Pass the needle through the next up bead on the first spiral and the first 2 beads on the second spiral. Work 1 B and 1 A. Work a sequence of 1 B, 2 B in one stitch, 1 B and 1 A for 4 times. End with 1 B, 2 B in one stitch, 1 B, 1 A.

ROW 12: String on 1 A bead and pass the needle through 2 up beads. Using B beads, work peyote stitch up the spiral, passing through both beads in the 2-drop stitches on the last row to add 21 beads in all.

ROW 13: Use your fingers to push the edge of all the other rows down below the beads on the first spiral so you have room to work the row.

Pass the needle through the next up bead on the first spiral and the first 2 beads on the second spiral. Work a sequence of 1 B, 1 B, 1 B, and 1 A for 4 times. End with 1 B, 1 B, and 1 B to add 19 beads in all.

ROW 14: String on 1 B bead and pass the needle through the first 2 up beads. Using B beads, peyote-stitch up the spiral to add 18 beads in all.

ROW 15: Pass through the next up bead on the first spiral and through the first 2 beads on the second spiral.

Work 1 B and 1 A. Work a sequence of 1 B, pass through 2, 1 B, and 1 A 3 times. End with 1 B and 1 B to add 13 beads.

ROW 16: String on 1 B bead and pass the needle through the first 2 up beads. Using B beads, peyote-stitch along the spiral to add 12 beads in all.

ROW 17: Pass the needle through the next up bead on the first spiral and through the first 2 beads on the second spiral. Work a sequence of 1 B, 1 B, and 1A for 3 times. End with 1 B to add 10 beads in all.

ROW 18: String on 1 B bead and pass the needle through the first 2 up beads. Work a sequence of 1 B, pass through 2 (to make a decrease), and 1 B 2 times. End with 1 B, 1 B, and 1 B to add 7 beads in all.

ROW 19: Pass the needle through the next up bead on the first spiral and the first up bead on the second spiral. Zip up the up beads of both spirals to close the work. Secure the thread and trim. If necessary, use an awl or darning needle to reshape the beadwork.

Tropical Bouquet Bead

Blue sea and bright tropical flowers combine in this lush Caribbean-flavored bead. Peyote-stitch flowers bloom in profusion on a herringbone-stitched tube.

DESIGNED BY
Carole Horn

TECHNIQUES
Herringbone stitch
Fringe
Peyote stitch

FINISHED SIZE
$1^{1}/_{4}$ x $1^{1}/_{2}$ inches
(3.1 x 3.8 cm)

MATERIALS & TOOLS

- Scissors
- Beading thread, size D
- Beading needle, size 10
- Japanese seed beads, size 11°, in dark blue for the base, green for the leaves, and several bright colors for the flower petals and stamen
- Small plastic coffee stirrer

1 With the scissors, cut a 1-yard (0.9 m) length of thread and pass it through the needle.

2 String on 4 blue beads and slide them 4 inches (10.2 cm) from the end of the thread. Pass the needle through all again to form a circle. With your fingers, manipulate the beads to make 2 stacks of beads sitting side by side. String on 2 blue beads and pass the needle down through the stack of beads just exited and up through the 2 just strung. Repeat to work a strip of ladder stitch 2 beads high and 6 beads long. Join the first and last stacks to make a foundation circle.

3 String on 2 blue beads and pass the needle down through the next bead on the foundation circle and up through the following one. Repeat around, working tubular herrinbone stitch, to add 6 beads in all. When you come to the end of the round, pass up through the next bead in the previous

round and the first bead added in this one to make a step up. (You will make a step up after each round.)

Repeat this step to work 4 more rounds.

4 Exiting from one of the beads at the top of the herringbone-stitched tube, string on 8 green beads. Skip the last bead strung and pass the needle back through the seventh bead. String on 5 green beads and pass the needle back through the first bead strung in this step and the bead exited at the beginning of this step. Pass the needle up through the next bead on the end of the tube (figure 1). Repeat to add 6 leaves around the top of the tube, but before you add leaves to the second side, slip a short length of the plastic coffee stirrer into the tube. Adding the leaves should pull in the tube a bit so the stirrer stays put; if not, then sew it into place.

Weave through the beads to exit from the other end of the beaded tube and repeat this step. Secure the thread and trim. Set the tube aside.

5 Cut a 1¼-yard (1.1 m) length of thread and pass it through the needle.

6 Make the tubular peyote-stitched flowers using the following round counts.

ROUNDS 1 AND 2: String on 5 base-color flower beads and slide them 4 inches (10.2 cm) from the end of the thread. Use a square knot to tie them into a circle. String on 1 base-color flower bead and pass the needle through the next bead in the

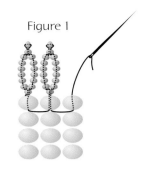

Figure 1

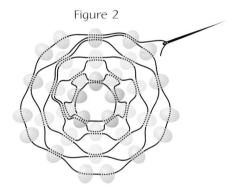

Figure 2

circle. Repeat around until you have 2 rounds with 5 beads in each round. Make a step up. You will step up after each round.

ROUNDS 3–5: Work 3 rounds of tubular peyote stitch using base-color flower beads to add 5 beads in each round.

ROUND 6: Work around in tubular peyote stitch, adding 2 base-color flower beads between each bead added in the previous round to make a series of increases. You will add 10 beads in all. Step up through the first bead added in the round (figure 2).

ROUND 7: Work around in tubular peyote stitch, adding 1 base-color

flower bead between each of the beads added in the previous round, to add 10 beads in all.

ROUND 8: Repeat Round 6 to add 20 beads in all. (The beadwork will begin to ruffle.)

ROUNDS 9 AND 10: Use contrasting-color flower beads and work in tubular peyote stitch to add 20 beads in each round.

Weave through the beads to exit from a bead on Round 1.

7 Pass up through the center of the flower. String on 7 base-color stamen beads and 3 contrasting-color stamen beads. Skip the last 3 beads strung and pass the needle back through the rest. Snug the beads and weave through several beads on the body of the flower. Exit from a bead on the first round and sew the flower to the side of the beaded tube. Secure the thread and trim.

8 Repeat steps 5 through 7 to make and add 2 more flowers to the beaded tube.

Gallery

Rebekah Hodous
Untitled, 2002
48.3 x 2.5 x 2.5 cm (necklace)
Cylinder seed beads, wooden beads, turquoise, brass, pewter clasp; two-drop peyote stitch
Photo © artist

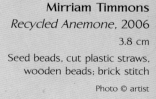

Mirriam Timmons
Recycled Anemone, 2006
3.8 cm
Seed beads, cut plastic straws, wooden beads; brick stitch
Photo © artist

Bird's Nest Bead

It seems that at any moment a tiny bird might peek out from within this nestlike bead. It's actually made of three layers of netting and is completely self-supporting.

DESIGNED BY
Gillian Lamb

TECHNIQUE
Netting

FINISHED SIZE
1 inch (2.5 cm)

- Scissors
- Beading thread, size D
- Beading needle, size 12
  Japanese seed beads in 2
  colors (A and C), size 11°
- Mandrel, skewer, or knitting
  needle (optional)
- Japanese triangle beads in 1
  color (B), size 10°

1 With the scissors, cut a 1½-yard (1.4 m) length of thread and pass it through the needle.

2 Work a base layer of tubular netting using the following round counts.

ROUND 1: String on 10 A beads and pass the needle through all again to make a tight foundation circle.

ROUND 2: String on 3 A beads, skip a bead on the foundation circle and, using firm thread tension, pass the needle through the next bead. Repeat around to add 15 beads in all (figure 1). Step up by passing through the first bead exited and up through the first 2 beads added in this round. (You will make this kind of step up after each round, exiting from the middle bead on the first net added in the previous round.)

ROUND 3: String on 5 A beads and pass the needle through the second (middle) bead on the next net added in the previous round. Repeat around to add 25 beads in all.

ROUND 4: Repeat Round 3, but add 5 A beads in each net to add 25 beads in all.

ROUND 5: Repeat Round 3, but add 7 A beads in each net to add 35 beads in all.

ROUND 6: Repeat Round 3, but add 7 A beads in each net to add 35 beads in all.

ROUND 7: Repeat Round 3, but add 5 A beads in each net to add 25 beads in all.

ROUND 8: Repeat Round 3, but add 5 A beads in each net to add 25 beads in all.

ROUND 9: Repeat Round 3, but add 3 A beads in each net to add 15 beads in all.

ROUND 10: Repeat Round 3, but add 1 A bead in each net, as in peyote stitch. You will add 5 beads in all. Exit from the last bead added and pull tight. Don't step up.

3 Work a second layer of tubular netting using the following round counts. If desired, place your beaded bead on the mandrel.

ROUND 1: String on 1 B bead and pass the needle through the next middle bead on a net in Round 9. Repeat around to add 5 B beads in all.

Pull tight. Weave through the beads to exit a middle bead on one of the nets in the next round of the first layer (figure 2).

ROUND 2: Repeat Round 1, but add 2 B beads in each net to add 10 beads in all.

ROUND 3: Repeat Round 1, but add 3 B beads in each net to add 15 beads in all.

ROUND 4: Repeat Round 1, but add 4 B beads in each net to add 20 beads in all.

ROUND 5: Repeat Round 1, but add 5 B beads in each net to add 25 beads in all.

ROUNDS 6–9: Repeat Rounds 4, 3, 2, and 1.

Weave through the beads to exit a bead in Round 9.

4 Work a third layer of tubular netting using the following round counts.

ROUNDS 1–9: String on 5 C beads and pass the needle through the beads added in the second layer. Repeat around to add 25 beads in all (figure 3). Weave down through the beads in the first layer and then pass the needle through a group of beads from the next round on the second layer.

5 Secure the thread and trim.

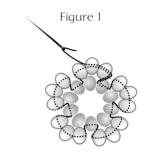

Figure 1

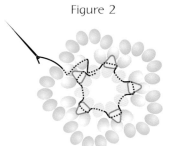

Figure 2

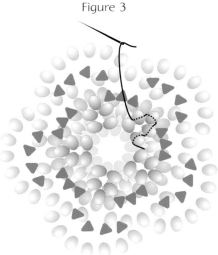

Figure 3

Warring States Bead

Long ago, the Chinese endured a period of time called "The Warring States," when many small kingdoms were eventually joined into seven larger ones. This beautifully embellished hair pipe bead was inspired by a map of the kingdoms, a juggernaut of sizes and shapes.

DESIGNED BY
D. Jeka Lambert

TECHNIQUE
Peyote stitch

FINISHED SIZE
**½ x 2¾ inch
(1.3 x 6.9 cm)**

1 With the scissors, cut a 3-yard (2.7 m) length of thread and pass it through one of the needles.

2 String on an even number of rocaille beads to fit snugly around the center of the hair pipe bead. Remove about half of the beads so that when they are evenly spaced around the hair pipe bead there is 1 bead width of space between them. Slide the beads 4 feet (120 cm) from the end of the thread. The long tail will be used later. Use a square knot to tie the beads into a circle around the hair pipe bead. Exit from the first bead strung. Slide the beadwork off of the hair pipe bead.

3 Using rocaille beads and firm thread tension, work tubular peyote stitch for 4 rounds. Step up after each round.

4 Slide the beadwork back onto the hair pipe bead and continue working tubular peyote stitch until the beadwork begins to feel slightly loose (about ½ inch [1.3 cm] from the end of the foundation bead). Set the working thread aside. Thread a second needle onto the tail thread and work tubular peyote stitch down to the other end of the hair pipe bead for the same amount of rounds as you did for the first half.

5 Make decreases as necessary to shape the beadwork so it remains snug against the hair pipe bead. To balance the shaping perfectly, make a decrease at one end of the hair pipe bead and then make a mirror decrease at the other end.

6 When you reach the end edge of the hair pipe bead, work 1 more round. Next, work decreases in every other stitch to shape the beadwork around the hair pipe bead's hole. In the following round, add 1 rocaille bead over each of the decreases. Weave several times through all the seed beads added in the last round to reinforce. Don't trim the thread if it's long enough to work the embellishments. Repeat for the other end of the foundation bead, but don't trim the thread.

7 Using 1 of the working threads, weave through the beads to exit from a bead at the center of the hair pipe bead.

8 Make the large embellishments using firm thread tension throughout. String on 1 size 8° bead and pass the needle through the bead just below the one just exited. To keep the size 8° bead from sitting askew, stitch through it again in the opposite direction to form an X in the center of it. String on 3 size 15° beads and pass the needle back through the bead you originally exited so the size 15° beads make a half circle around the size 8° bead (figure 1). Repeat to make another half circle on the other side of the size 8° bead.

Figure 1

97

Weave through the beads to exit from the bead that lies just above the size 8° bead, passing the needle through it from left to right. String on 7 size 15° beads, wrap around the half circle on the right side of the size 8° bead, and pass the needle through the bead just below the size 8° bead, passing from right to left. Repeat on the left side of the size 8° bead to make another large half circle that hugs the small half circle. For the half circles to stay in position, you need to work with very firm thread tension.

Add 2 more large embellishments to the horizontal row, spacing them as evenly as possible around the hair pipe bead.

9 Weave through the beads to exit midway between the embellishment you just made and the end of the hair pipe bead, directly above the embellishment. Add another set of 3 large embellishments horizontally around the bead, each placed directly above the one stitched before. Make another set of 3 large embellishments on the other end of the hair pipe bead to mirror this set's placement.

10 Make the small embellishments. Weave through the beads to exit from a foundation bead on the fifth row. The bead should lie on a vertical row that's midway between the large embellishments. String on 1 size 11° seed bead and stitch it onto the bead you just exited. String on 3 size 15° beads and stitch them onto the bead just exited. Pull firmly so the size 15° beads hug the bottom of the size 11° bead. String on 4 size 15° beads and stitch them onto the bead just exited. Pull firmly so they hug the top of the size 11° bead. The embellishments should look like small flowers.

Add 2 more small embellishments to the horizontal row, spacing them as evenly as possible around the hairpipe bead.

11 Weave through the beads to exit about one-third of the way up the hair pipe bead, directly above a small bead embellishment. Add another set of 3 small embellishments, each placed directly above the one stitched before. Weave another set of 3 small embellishments two-thirds of the way up the hair pipe bead and another set at a point that mirrors the first set's placement. Secure the thread and trim.

Gallery

Lisa Gastelum

Fall Foliage and Fringe, 2005

47.6 cm long (necklace)

Seed beads, wooden beads, sterling silver; gourd stitch, fringe

Photos © Eric Griswold

Jo Lessa Willey

Snood Beads, 2005

15 x 18 cm

Seed beads, round beads; netting

Photo © Richard Reid

Firecracker Beads

These unique beads virtually explode with color and texture—no wonder they're called "firecracker!" The fringe used at either end of these beads is unique, too; the designer calls it "sparkle fringe."

DESIGNED BY
Yoshie Marubashi

TECHNIQUES
Peyote stitch
Fringe

FINISHED SIZE
1⅛ x 1¾ inches
(2.9 x 4.4 cm)

MATERIALS & TOOLS

- Scissors
- Beading thread, size B
- Beading needle, size 12
- Beeswax
- Japanese cylinder beads in 2 colors (A and B)
- Large tube bead, $^5/_{16}$ x $^{13}/_{16}$ inch (6 x 21 mm)
- Seed beads, size 8° (C)
- Seed beads, size 14° (D)
- Seed beads, size 11° (E)

1 With the scissors, cut a 10-foot (3 m) length of beading thread and pass it through the needle. Double the thread so the ends match and wax. Add a stop bead to the end of the thread, leaving a 4-inch (10.2 cm) tail.

2 Following one of the charts in figure 1, string on the A and B beads designated for rows 1 and 2. Work the rest of the chart (28 rows) in flat even-count peyote stitch. Bend the beadwork so the first and last rows touch, insert the large tube bead, and zip up the beadwork to make a tube. Remove the stop bead and use the tail and working thread to tie a square knot.

3 With the thread exiting from the end of the beaded tube, string on 1 A, 1 C, and 1 A. Skip 1 bead along the edge of the tube, and pass under the exposed thread between the next 2 beads on the edge (figure 2). Repeat, adding 21 beads in all.

4 Working off the first C bead added in the previous step, make the sparkle fringe. String on 4 D, 1 E, 1 D, 1 E, and 1 D. Skipping the last 3 beads, pass the needle back through the first E bead just strung.

String on 4 D, 1 E, 1 D, 1 E, and 1 D. Skipping the last 3 beads, pass the needle back through the first E bead just strung. String on 4 D beads and pass the needle through the C bead you last exited.

Repeat this step three times so you end up with 4 triangles coming off of the C bead. Note in figure 3 how the thread passes through the C bead for each of fringes 1 through 4. It's important to follow this thread path, or your fringe won't turn out correctly.

Weave through the A beads on the beaded tube so you exit from the next C bead.

5 Repeat step 4 to add sparkle fringe on each of the C beads at the edge of the tube.

6 Weave through the beads to the other side of the tube and repeat steps 3 through 5. Secure the thread and trim.

Figure 1

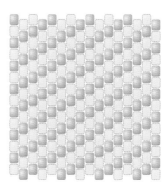

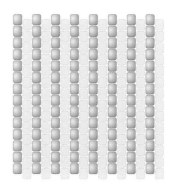

Figure 2

Figure 3

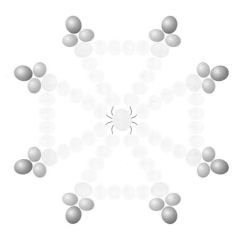

Tablet Bead

This bead contains a surprise: an interior layer of color when you hold it up to the light. Because it's made with right-angle weave, this lacy bead is full of holes, so you can string it any which way and it still looks fabulous.

DESIGNED BY
Christine Prussing

TECHNIQUE
Right-angle weave

FINISHED SIZE
$^3/_4$ x $^3/_4$ x $^1/_2$ inch
(1.9 x 1.9 x 1.3 cm)

Figure 1

Start

Figure 2

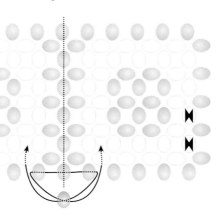

1 With the scissors, cut a 1-yard (0.9 m) length of thread and thread 1 needle on each end.

2 Following figure 1, and using the opal white size 10° beads, work five 11-unit rows of double-needle right-angle weave, ending with one or two concealed square knots inside the beads shown. Trim the thread ends with the thread burner.

3 Rotate your work 90 degrees so it's oriented as in figure 2. Anchor the remaining thread so it exits the turquoise "hinge" bead and adjacent white opal beads indicated in the illustration. String on 1 turquoise bead on 1 thread end and pass the other thread end back through it.

4 Pass each thread end through the adjacent crystal beads indicated in figure 3, continuing to join

Figure 3

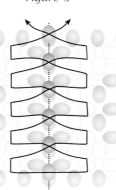

Figure 4

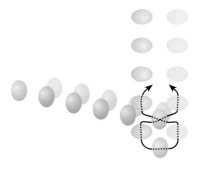

Figure 5

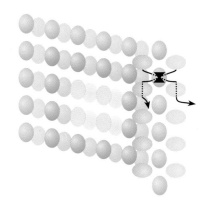

the bead's interior. When you reach the corner, pass 1 thread end in a figure eight around the edge beads as shown in figure 4. Pass the other thread end through the next edge bead as shown.

5 Join the second interior row (it runs parallel to the first interior row) with a turquoise edge bead, followed by a kelly-sapphire-sapphire-kelly-turquoise sequence. Make a figure eight as before at the end of this row.

6 Repeat step 5 to join the third interior row. Repeat step 4 to join the fourth interior row. Finish with an edge row of turquoise, working the threads around the corner of the tablet and tying a concealed square knot inside the first turquoise bead from the corner. Pass each thread through the next adjacent white opal bead on their respective edges (figure 5).

7 Using each thread end on their respective perimeters of the tablet, string on 1 size 14° bead and pass the needle through the next white opal edge bead. Continue around, adding 1 size 14° bead between each edge bead.

8 Finish by passing each thread again through the starting white opal bead, then tying a concealed square knot inside the turquoise bead at the center of the edge, second from the corner. To make sure they're secure, work the thread ends through the next white opal edge beads (not the size 14° seed beads) and tie another concealed square knot inside the third turquoise bead from the corner. Trim the ends with the thread burner.

These versatile beads can be strung in a variety of ways to complete any type of jewelry design.

Gallery

Lisa Gastelum
Cocktail Time, 2005
3 x 4.2 x 2.5 cm

Seed beads, wooden beads, pearls, sterling silver; gourd stitch, wirework

Photo © Eric Griswold

Jóh Ricci
Triangle Necklace, 1999
2.5 x 0.6 cm (beads), 26 x 14.6 cm (necklace)

Cylinder seed beads, sterling silver and gold-filled beads and findings; gourd stitch

Photo © T. R. Wailles

Feather Bead

A stylized feather design makes this beaded bead fly. You stitch the feather separately using a combination of right-angle weave, peyote stitch, and simple fringe, and then sew it to a peyote-stitched band.

DESIGNED BY
Paula Parmenter

TECHNIQUES:
**Right-angle weave
Peyote stitch
Fringe**

FINISHED SIZE
**$1/2$ x 1 inch
(1.2 x 2.5 cm)**

1 With the scissors, cut a 1½-yard (1.4 m) length of thread. Condition it and pass it through the needle.

2 String on 4 A beads and slide them 12 inches (30.5 cm) from the end of the thread. Pass the needle through the first 3 beads just strung to form a circle.

3 With A beads, work single needle right-angle weave until you have a strip 9 units long and 1 unit wide.

4 Weave through the beads and exit from a side bead on the eighth unit. String on 11 A beads and pass the needle through the bead opposite the one you just exited (figure 1) to make a base loop around the eighth and ninth units.

5 String on 1 B bead and pass the needle through the bead on the right side of the seventh unit. Repeat down the strip, adding 1 B bead between each side bead. When you reach the last side bead, pass the needle through the end and left-side beads of the first unit. As you did down the right side of the strip, add 1 B bead between each side bead up the left side of the strip.

6 Weave through the base loop made in step 4 and exit from the sixth bead. Pass the needle through the end bead on the ninth unit, and then through the sixth loop bead again (figure 2). This is the bottom of the feather.

MATERIALS & TOOLS

- Scissors
- Beading thread, size B
- Thread conditioner
- Beading needle, size 13
- Seed beads in 2 colors (A and B), size 15°
- Japanese cylinder beads

Figure 1

Figure 2

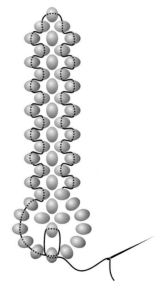

Figure 3

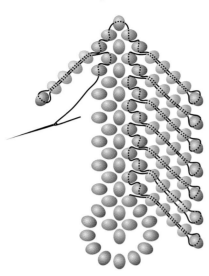

7 Weave through the beads to exit from the side bead of the second unit. String on 4 B beads and 1 A bead. Skip the last bead and pass the needle back through the 4 B beads just strung. Pass the needle through the first bead added in step 5 *from the bottom to the top* of the feather (this is important for the fringe to be positioned correctly), and the side bead on the following unit. Repeat, adding simple fringe legs along the right side of the feather. When you reach the last bead on the right side, weave through the 3 end beads on the first unit and continue making fringe legs along the left side (figure 3). *Note:* When you add fringe to the left side of the feather, you'll enter the step 5 beads from the top to the bottom, and then reenter them from the bottom to the top.

8 Weave through the beads to exit from the sixth bead on the base loop. Don't cut the threads. Set the feather aside.

9 Repeat steps 1 through 8 to make another feather.

10 Cut a 1-yard (.9 m) length of thread, condition it, and pass it through the needle.

11 Use the cylinder beads to make a strip of flat even-count peyote-stitch 10 beads wide and 58 rows long (there will be 29 beads along each of the long edges).

Bend the strip so the first and last rows touch and zip them up. Secure the thread and trim. With your fingers, press the band flat.

12 Center one of the feathers on the flat side of the band. Use the feather's working and tail threads to stitch its center to the band's center beads.

13 Weave through the band's beads to exit from an edge bead that matches up with a feather tip. Stitch the 2 beads together. Repeat down the feather to secure all the tips. *Note:* The feather tips are sewn to the edge beads only, and, because of the difference in bead widths, the beads won't match up exactly. You'll need to judge which edge bead to use for which tip. Repeat on the other side of the feather. Secure the thread and trim.

14 Repeat step 13 to secure the other feather to the other flat side of the band.

Gallery

Margo C. Field
Floresta Opus Two "Elsinor", 2005
5.7 x 3.2 x 3.2 cm
Seed beads, vintage sequins; peyote stitch
Photo © Pat Berrett

Beading Heart Bead

If your heart beats for beads, this one's for you! This challenging project assumes you have a firm handle on double-needle right-angle weave, but the results are amazing: a three-dimensional heart bead that's woven together in one piece, using a single length of line and just one knot.

DESIGNED BY
Christine Prussing

TECHNIQUE
Right-angle weave

FINISHED SIZE
1 x $^7/_8$ x $^1/_2$ inch
(2.5 x 2.2 x 1.3 cm)

MATERIALS & TOOLS

- Permanent markers, red and black

- 1 yard (0.9 m) of 8-pound (3.6 kg) test monofilament line

- 63 bicone crystal beads, $^3/_{16}$ inch (4 mm) each

- Beading tweezers

- Scissors

- Thread burner

Figure 1

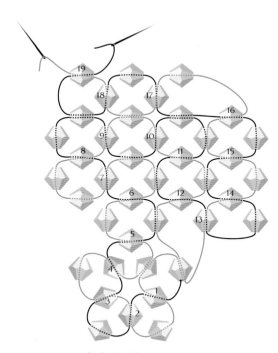

[Lobe 1, Side 1, Rim]

1 The heart is worked with double-needle right-angle weave. To maintain your orientation and to follow the diagram steps more easily, use permanent markers to color one end of your line red, and the other black. The red thread paths on the illustrations show the thread path for the red end, the black paths for the black end.

Note: In the following weave instructions, "red" refers to the red thread end, and "black" refers to the black thread end. The last thread listed always passes back through ("crosses") the last bead strung, unless otherwise indicated.

2 Following figure 1, use the bicone beads to make Lobe 1. Always pull the thread snug so the beads curve upward into a bowl (it's important that they not curve downward into a dome).

WEAVE 1: Red strings on 3 beads; black crosses.

WEAVE 2: Red strings on 2 beads; black crosses.

WEAVE 3: Black strings on 2 beads; red crosses.

WEAVE 4: Red strings on 2 beads; black crosses.

WEAVE 5: Red passes back through the second bead strung in Weave 1. Red strings on 1 bead; black crosses. You should now have a star shape ("Lobe 1").

3 Continue to work the inner and outer edges of Side 1, connecting its outer edge to Lobe 1 at weave 13.

WEAVE 6: Red strings on 1 bead; black strings on 2 beads; red crosses.

WEAVE 7: Red strings on 3 beads; black crosses.

WEAVE 8: Red strings on 3 beads; black crosses.

WEAVE 9: Black strings on 3 beads; red crosses.

WEAVE 10: Black passes back through the second bead strung in Weave 7. Red strings on 2 beads; black crosses.

WEAVE 11: Black strings on 3 beads; red crosses.

WEAVE 12: Black passes back through the first bead strung in Weave 7. Red strings on 2 beads; black crosses.

WEAVE 13: Red passes back through the first bead strung on black in Weave 6 and the first bead strung in Weave 1. Red strings on 1 bead; black crosses. Pull tight. The heart's lobe (Weaves 1 through 5) will fold over on the rest of the weaves.

WEAVE 14: Black strings on 2 beads; red crosses.

WEAVE 15: Black passes back through the first bead strung in Weave 12. Red strings on 2 beads; black crosses.

WEAVE 16: Red passes back through the second bead strung in Weave 11. Black strings on 2 beads; red crosses.

WEAVE 17: Black passes back through the first bead strung in Weave 11. Red strings on 2 beads; black crosses.

WEAVE 18: Red passes back through the first bead strung in Weave 10. Black strings on 2 beads; red crosses.

WEAVE 19: Black passes back through the second bead strung in Weave 9 and strings on 1 bead; red crosses.

4 Rotate your work 180 degrees to follow figure 2. This section creates the outer and inner edges of Side 2.

WEAVE 20: Red strings on 3 beads; black crosses.

WEAVE 21: Red passes back through the first bead strung in Weave 18. Black strings on 2 beads; red crosses.

WEAVE 22: Black passes back through the first bead strung in Weave 17, the first bead strung in Weave 16, and strings on 1 bead; red crosses.

WEAVE 23: Red passes back through the first bead strung in Weave 15. Black strings on 2 beads; red crosses.

WEAVE 24: Black passes back through the first bead strung in Weave 14 and the first bead strung on black in Weave 3 (a lobe bead). Black strings on 1 bead; red crosses.

WEAVE 25: Red passes back through the first bead strung in Weave 2 (a lobe bead) and strings on 2 beads; black crosses.

WEAVE 26: Red passes through the first bead strung in Weave 23, the first bead strung in Weave 21, and strings on 1 bead; black crosses.

WEAVE 27: Black passes through the second bead strung in Weave 20. Red strings on 2 beads; black crosses.

5 Make Lobe 2, pulling the thread snug so that it resembles a dome or an overturned bowl (just the opposite of Lobe 1).

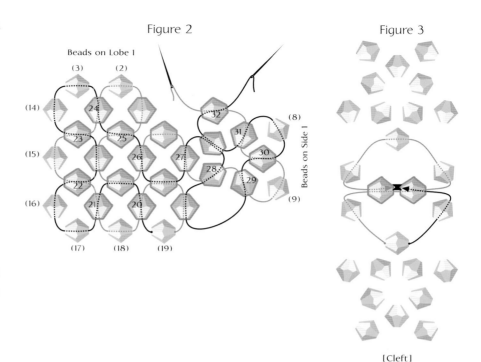

Figure 2

Beads on Lobe 1

(3) (2)

(14)

(15)

(16)

(17) (18) (19)

Beads on Side 1

(8)

(9)

Figure 3

[Cleft]

WEAVE 28: Black strings on 2 beads; red crosses.

WEAVE 29: Black passes back through the first bead strung in Weave 20 and strings on 1 bead; red crosses.

WEAVE 30: Red passes back through the first bead strung in Weave 9 and strings on 1 bead; black crosses.

WEAVE 31: Black passes back through the second bead strung in Weave 8 and strings on 1 bead; red crosses.

WEAVE 32: Black passes back through the second bead strung in Weave 28 and strings on 1 bead; red crosses.

6 Turn the beadwork so the lobes are on top. You will now add the cleft beads that act as the joist for the center of the heart.

Weave through the beads to exit as shown in figure 3. Follow the figure carefully to see the thread path.

WEAVE 33: Red passes back through the adjacent bead shown, strings on 2 beads, passes through the diagonally opposite side bead shown, through the opposite lobe bead, through the adjacent side bead, and again through one of the center beads. Black passes back through the adjacent side bead and through one center bead.

7 Secure the thread with a surgeon's knot, trim with the scissors, and melt the tails. With the beading tweezers, press the two cleft beads down inside the heart to make it bulge outward.

Pom-Pom Bead

This bead looks just like the fuzzy pom-poms you might find on a winter hat or a pair of roller skates—but this version is made of glass. It's done by first covering a base bead with peyote stitch, and then working fringe right off the beads.

DESIGNED BY
Nancy Zellers

TECHNIQUES
Peyote stitch
Fringe

FINISHED SIZE
1⅝ inches (4.3 cm)

- Base bead, $\frac{3}{4}$ inch (1.9 cm), of wood, plastic, resin, or gesso-covered polystyrene foam
- Permanent markers or paint to color the base bead
- Scissors
- Beading thread to match base bead color, size B
- Thread conditioner
- Beading needle, size 10 or 12
- Seed beads, size 11°
- Double-sided tape (optional)
- Skewer or toothpick

1 Color the base bead with permanent marker or paint to match the seed beads. Let the coloring dry.

2 With the scissors, cut a 1-yard (.9 m) length of beading thread, condition it, and pass it through the needle.

3 String on enough beads to fit snugly around the equator of your base bead, and slide them 4 inches (10.2 cm) from the end of the thread. Tie the working and tail threads in a square knot, and slide the foundation circle onto the base bead. If desired, first wrap the base bead's equator with double-sided tape and place the foundation circle over the tape. This may help you keep the beads in place as you work.

4 Work around the foundation circle in tubular peyote stitch, making decreases as necessary, until you reach the base bead's hole. Make sure you step up after each round. After the first few rounds, you'll need to make one or more decreases on each round.

Finish this half of the bead by passing the needle through the up beads of the last round. Pull snugly to make a neat ring. Secure the thread and trim.

5 Put a skewer through the base bead's hole to help keep the beads from sliding around as you work the other half of the base bead.

6 Start a new thread that exits a bead on the foundation circle. Cover the second half of the base bead the same way you worked the first half, decreasing as necessary, and ending in a neat ring around the bead hole. Secure the thread and trim.

7 Start a new thread and make simple fringe legs, each 4 to 6 beads long, off of the seed beads you stitched in steps 1–6. The fringes can all be the same length or varied. Secure the thread and trim.

VARIATIONS

For an interesting variation, create a peyote-stitched pattern (i.e., spirals, vertical stripes, horizontal bands) with the seed beads stitched in steps 1–6. Then, when you make your fringe, echo the color of those initial stitched beads to preserve the pattern.

To make a spiky-looking bead, use cylinder beads instead of seed beads and add fringe to only half of the seed beads stitched in steps 1–6. Vary the fringe length from 6 beads to 9 beads to increase the spiky look.

Baroque Bead

This stunning bead's flamboyant and fantastic design definitely qualifies it as baroque. Using herringbone stitch with exaggerated increases, you create two umbrella shapes and then connect them.

DESIGNED BY
Carole Horn

TECHNIQUE
Herringbone stitch

FINISHED SIZE
$1^3/_4$ x 1 inch
(4.4 x 2.5 cm)

1 With the scissors, cut a 2-yard (1.8 m) length of thread and pass it through the needle.

2 Make a ladder-stitched base circle (Rounds 1 and 2). String on 4 A beads and slide them 18 inches (45 cm) from the end of the thread. Pass the needle through all again. Manipulate the beads so you have 2 stacks of 2 beads sitting side by side. String on 2 A beads and pass the needle down through the last 2 beads strung and up through the 2 beads just strung. Repeat until you have a strip 6 beads long and 2 beads tall. Join the first and last stacks to make a foundation circle. Your tail and working threads should exit from opposite sides on the first stack.

3 Make rounds of tubular herringbone stitch, following the counts below.

ROUND 3: String on 2 A beads and pass the needle down through the top A bead on the next stack and up through the top bead on the following stack. Repeat around to add 6 beads in all. At the end of the round, step up by passing the needle up through the next bead on the previous round and the first bead added in the round. (You'll step up after each round.)

ROUND 4: String on 2 A beads and pass the needle down through the next A bead from the previous round. String on 1 B bead and pass the needle up through the next bead to make an increase. Repeat around to add 3 pairs of A beads with 1 B bead between each pair (6 A, 3 B in all).

ROUND 5: String on 2 A beads and pass the needle down through the next bead from the previous round. String on 2 B beads and pass the needle up through the next A bead from the previous round. Repeat around to add 3 pairs of A beads with 2 B beads between each pair (6 A, 6 B in all).

ROUND 6: String on 2 A beads and pass the needle down through the next A bead from the previous round and up through the next B bead. String on 2 B beads, then pass the

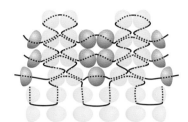

Figure 1

needle down through the next B bead and up through the following A bead (figure 1). Repeat around to add 3 pairs of A and 3 pairs of B (6 A, 6 B in all). The work will begin to look the spokes of a wheel.

ROUND 7: String on 2 A beads and pass the needle down through the next A bead on the previous round. String on 1 C bead and pass the needle up through the next B bead. String on 2 B beads and pass the needle down through the next B bead. String on 1 C bead and pass the needle up through the next A bead. Repeat around to add 1 C bead between each spoke (6 A, 6 B, 6 C in all).

ROUND 8: Repeat Round 7, but add 2 C beads between each spoke (24 beads in all).

ROUNDS 9–12: Repeat Round 7, increasing 1 C bead in each section between the spokes until you have 6 spokes with 6 C beads between each.

ROUND 13: With the thread exiting the first bead at the end of a spoke, string on 1 size 11° bead that is the contrasting color of the spoke. Pass the needle down into the next bead, through the 6 C beads between the spokes, and up through top bead of the next spoke (figure 2). Repeat around to add 6 beads in all. Secure the thread and trim.

4 Make the second half of the beaded bead. Repeat step 3, Rounds 1–12 (omit Round 13). Don't trim the thread.

5 Match the 2 beaded halves so the same color spokes are together. With the second half's working thread exiting from the first bead of a spoke, pass the needle through the corresponding bead added in Round 13 of the first half. Pass the needle down into the next bead on the second half, through the adjacent 6 C beads, and up through the top bead on the following spoke (figure 3). Repeat until the 2 halves are joined. Secure the thread and trim.

6 Make the end embellishments. Turn the beaded bead so one of the ends is up. Using the tail thread on that end, weave through the beads to exit out from the first bead of a pair that corresponds with one of the A spokes. Repeat Rounds 3 (figure 4) and 4. Repeat Round 5, but add 3 B beads between the spokes instead of 2. Repeat Round 13 using all A beads. Secure the thread and trim.

7 Repeat step 6 to embellish the other end of the beaded bead.

Figure 2

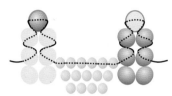

Figure 3

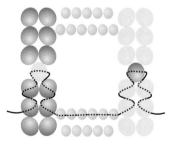

Figure 4

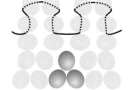

Thom Atkins
Rouge et Noir, 2006
17.5 x 4 cm (pendant unit), 88 cm long (necklace)
Seed beads, wooden beads, wire; peyote stitch
Photo © artist

Gallery

JoAnn Baumann
Bead Happy, 2004

40.6 cm long (necklace)

Seed beads, lampworked discs;
right-angle weave over bead forms

Photo © Larry Sanders

Miriam Timmons
Recycled Planet, 2006

3.8 cm

Seed beads, cut plastic straws, wooden
beads; brick stitch

Photo © artist

Double Dutch Bead

This soft, airy bead's spirals swirl like two jumpropes in a game of Double Dutch gone wild. The designer conceived the construction while making swatches for a Dutch Spirals class she was teaching—by simply making quick increases and decreases, a beaded bead was born.

DESIGNED BY
Kathy Seely

TECHNIQUE
Netting

FINISHED SIZE
1 3/16 x 7/8 inch
(3 x 2.2 cm)

MATERIALS & TOOLS

Scissors

Beading thread to match size 11° beads, size D

Beading needle, size 10 or 13

Japanese seed beads in color A, size 11°

Accent beads for spiral in color B, sizes 9° through 6°

Long needle or skewer (optional)

Florist's foam block (optional)

Small paintbrush (optional)

TIPS

- Try different bead sizes and types to vary the look.

- Make the bead rigid by coating it with acrylic floor wax. This is useful if you are stringing the beaded bead with other beads in such a way that it needs to keep its shape. It ensures that stringing wire or thread will be hidden.

1 With the scissors, cut a 1-yard (0.9 m) length of thread and pass it through the needle.

2 Work the following rounds of tubular netting. Keep your tension very tight throughout.

ROUND 1: String on 1 A, 1 B, 1 A, 1 B, 1 A, and 1 B. Pass the needle through all the beads twice more to make a tight circle. Exit from any B bead.

ROUND 2: String on 2 A and 1 B. Pass the needle through the next B bead. Repeat around to add 9 beads in all. Make the step up by weaving through the beads to exit from the first B bead

added in this round. (You'll make this step up after every round.)

ROUND 3: String on 3 A and 1 B. Pass the needle through the next B bead added in the previous round. Repeat around to add 12 beads in all.

Note: In all the rounds there will be 2 B beads right next to each other. To find the correct one to pass through, choose the one that has the amount of size 11° beads you added in each stitch on the previous round. So, for this round, it would be the B bead with the 2 A beads right before it (figure 1).

ROUND 4: String on 4 A and 1 B and pass the needle through the next B bead added in the previous round. Repeat around to add 15 beads in all.

ROUND 5: String on 5 A and 1 B and pass the needle through the next B bead added in the previous round. Repeat around to add 18 beads in all.

ROUND 6: String on 6 A and 1 B and pass the needle through the next B bead added in the previous round. Repeat around to add 21 beads in all.

ROUND 7: String on 7 A and 1 B and pass the needle through the next B bead added in the previous round. Repeat around to add 24 beads in all.

ROUND 8: String on 8 A and 1 B and pass the needle through the next B bead added in the previous round. Repeat around to add 27 beads in all.

Figure 1

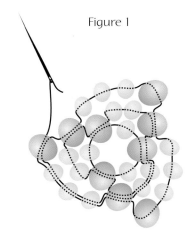

ROUND 9: This is the middle of the beaded bead. String on 9 A and 1 B and pass the needle through the next B bead added in the previous round. Repeat around to add 30 beads in all.

3 To finish working the bead, work the counts for Rounds 8 through 1 (reverse order).

4 Weave through the last round twice to reinforce the bead. Secure the working and tail threads and trim.

5 If desired, stiffen the beaded bead by sliding it onto a long needle or skewer and inserting the needle or skewer horizontally into a block of florist's foam. Using a small paintbrush, paint the bead with a coat of acrylic floor wax, and let it dry for at least 3 hours. Repeat until the desired degree of rigidity is reached.

Gallery

JoAnn Baumann
Brights Galore, 2005
51.8 cm long (necklace)
Seed beads, pressed glass beads; right-angle weave (some over bead forms)
Photo © artist

Lisa Gastelum
Flower Buds, 2005
2.7 x 2 x 1.4 cm
Seed beads, wooden beads, sterling silver; gourd stitch, wirework
Photo © Eric Griswold

Puffy Mandala Bead

Deserving of deep meditation by any appreciative beader, this blissful beaded bead carries an inner secret: its stuffing! Common kitchen plastic wrap fluffs up a pair of flat, circular peyote-stitched hexagons to make a single squishy bead.

DESIGNED BY
Mary Tafoya

TECHNIQUE
Peyote stitch

FINISHED SIZE
1 x ⅜ inch (2.5 x 1 cm)

- Scissors

- Beading thread, size B

- Beading needle, size 10

- Japanese cylinder beads in 5 contrasting colors: white-lined crystal AB, transparent Capri blue AB, matte metallic dark raspberry iris, variegated taupe silk satin, opaque antique rose

- Strip of clear plastic kitchen wrap, 2 x 10 inches (5.1 x 25 cm)

- Small knitting needle, beading awl, or any thin sturdy tool

TIPS

- If you design your own pattern, keep in mind that when strung, the edge of the beaded bead will show more than the center—so make the outer rows sparkly and interesting.

- When incorporating your Puffy Mandalas into beadwork jewelry, just poke the beading needle through the plastic wrap and keep stringing.

1 With the scissors, cut a 1-yard (0.9 m) length of thread and pass it through the needle.

2 Make a flat hexagon using circular peyote stitch. See figure 1 for bead placement. The chart indicates each round by number. Increases are marked in bold. (Stitch Round 14 only on the second disk.)

ROUND 1: String on 6 taupe beads and slide them 4 inches (10.2 cm) from the end of the thread. Use a square knot to tie the beads in a circle. Exit from the first bead strung.

ROUND 2: String on 1 antique rose bead and pass the needle through the next bead from Round 1. Repeat around to add 6 beads in all. Step up to begin the next round. (You will step up after every round.)

ROUND 3: This is an increase round. String on 2 antique rose beads and pass the needle through the next bead from the previous round. Repeat around to add 12 beads in all. Exit between the first two beads added in this round.

ROUND 4: String on 1 white-lined crystal and pass the needle through the next bead added in the previous round. Repeat around to add 12 beads in all. *Note:* When you come to the bead pairs from the previous round, you'll need to pull the thread snug to force the new bead between the pair.

ROUNDS 5–13: Continue working in circular peyote stitch, making increases as you did in Round 3 in Rounds 6, 9, and 12. Split the increases in Rounds 7, 10, and 13. Follow figure 1 for color

placement or create your own. Secure the thread and trim.

3 Repeat step 2 to make a second mandala. Add 1 more round so it has 14 rounds in all. Don't trim the thread.

Note: If you decide to make your beaded bead smaller or larger, avoid ending at an increase round. When joining the two sides together in the next step, it's easiest if the smaller of the two hexagons ends at a round that splits the increases and the larger one ends at a normal round.

4 Match up the two hexagons so the corners are together. Use firm thread tension to zip up the beads until you're about three-fourths of the way around. Use the knitting needle to stuff the plastic strip into the bead, making sure it's evenly distributed. Cut and add more plastic wrap if needed. Use the tool to tuck in the last bits of plastic while you zip up the rest of the edging. Secure the thread and trim.

Figure 1

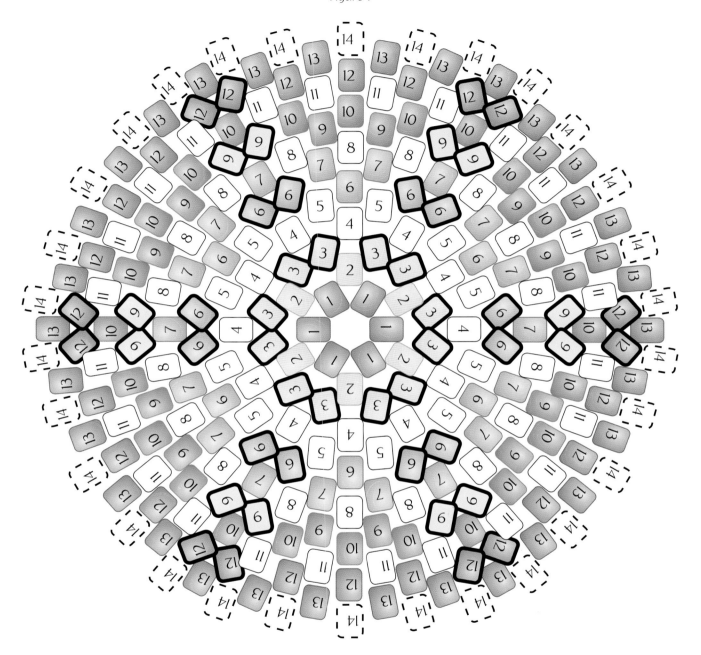

CHART NOTES

- Numbers indicate rounds.
- Bold-outlined beads indicate increases.
- Round 14 is made only on the second disk.

Smocked Bead

Reminiscent of an elaborate spinning ballroom crystal, this awe-inspiring bead is made using a technique that mimics fabric smocking. Especially effective on large round or oval beads, the result is a bold attention-getter.

DESIGNED BY
Joanne Waters

TECHNIQUE
Netting

FINISHED SIZE
$1\frac{3}{4}$ x $1\frac{1}{2}$ inches
(4.4 x 3.8 cm)

1 With the scissors, cut a 1½-yard (1.4 m) length of thread and pass it through a needle.

2 String on 28 A beads and slide them 4 inches (10.2 cm) from the end of the thread. Use a square knot to tie the beads into a base circle. Pass the needle through all the beads again. Slip the base circle and the wooden bead onto the dowel.

MATERIALS & TOOLS

- Scissors
- Beading thread, size D
- Beading needle, size 10 or 11
- Japanese cylinder beads (A)
- 1¼-inch (3.1 cm) round painted wooden bead with a ½-inch (1.3 cm) hole
- ½-inch (1.3 cm) diameter dowel or knitting needle that fits snugly inside the wooden bead's hole
- Seed beads in size 11° (B)
- Tube-shaped seed beads in size 10° (C)
- 56 round Czech fire-polished beads, each 3/16 inch (4 mm)

3 String on 5 B beads. String on 1 C and 3 B five times. String on 1 C and 5 B. The strand of beads should stretch from one end of the wooden bead to the other. If the strand is too short or too long, add or subtract beads to the first and last 5 B.

4 String on 28 A. Wrap these beads around the dowel at the other end of the wooden bead. Pass the needle through all the A beads again to make a second base circle (figure 1) and exit from the first bead strung.

5 Repeat step 3 to make another strand of beads, this time passing through the corresponding cylinder bead at the other end of the wooden bead. Continue adding strands of beads until you've connected each bead on one base circle to those on the other one. You will add 28 strands in all.

6 Weave through one of the strands to exit from the eleventh bead up from the first C strung. String on 1 fire-polished bead and pass through the eleventh bead on the next strand. String on 1 B bead and pass through the eleventh bead on the next strand. Repeat around (figure 2) to add 28 beads in all.

Note: Because seed and fire-polished beads vary in size, you may need to adjust the amount added between the strands to make a snug fit around the wooden bead's circumference.

Figure 1

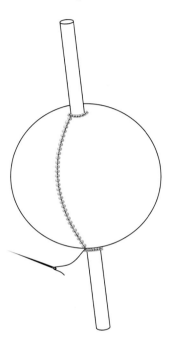

Figure 2

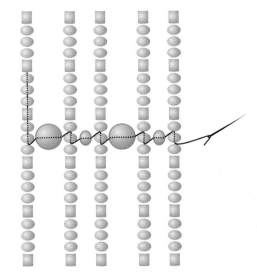

7 Weave through one of the strands where you added a B bead on the right and a fire-polished bead on the left in the previous step. Exit from the 15th bead up from the first C bead strung. String on 1 fire-polished bead and pass through the 15th bead on the next strand. (The bead should end up over a size 10° bead placed in the previous step.) Repeat around to add 14 beads in all.

8 Weave through one of the strands where, when you exit from the nineteenth bead, you'll be positioned over one of the fire-polished beads added in step 6. String on 1 fire-polished bead and pass the needle through the nineteenth beads on the next two strands. String on 1 B bead and pass the needle through the 19th bead on the next two strands. Repeat around to add 14 beads in all.

9 Repeat steps 7 and 8 to make mirror smocking rounds on the opposite side of the beaded bead. Secure the working and tail threads and trim. Remove the dowel from the bead.

Gallery

Margo C. Field
Floresta Opus One "Ophelia", 2005
2.5 x 5.7 x 2.5 cm
Seed beads, freshwater pearls; peyote stitch, fringe
Photo © Pat Berrett

Mirriam Timmons
Link Necklaces, 2005
40.6 cm long
Seed beads, chain links, rubber cord; brick stitch
Photo © artist

Crystal Sleeve Bead

This tubular bead comes with an added bonus: tassels! When you string the crystal tube, you can create instant dangles for a fabulous focal point on a necklace.

DESIGNED BY
Nancy Zellers

TECHNIQUES
Right-angle weave
Fringe
Peyote stitch
Square stitch

FINISHED SIZE
6½ inches (16.5 cm)

TO MAKE THE SLEEVE BEAD

1 With the scissors, cut a 2-yard (1.8 m) length of beading thread, condition it, and pass it through the needle.

2 Make a strip of flat single-needle right-angle weave 8 units wide by 9 units long. Use the crystals to form the sides of the right-angle weave units and 2 seed beads to form the top and bottom of each unit (figure 1). Set aside.

3 If desired, make the double-ended tassel as described below to place within the sleeve bead. Lay the tassels across the cylinder bead strip (figure 2).

4 Fold the strip so the short sides meet and stitch all of the first and last units together to form a tube (figure 3).

5 Weave through the beads to exit from a pair of seed beads at the top of the tube. String on 1 seed bead, pass through the next pair of seed beads, and pull snug. Continue around to form a solid ring of seed beads. Secure the threads and trim.

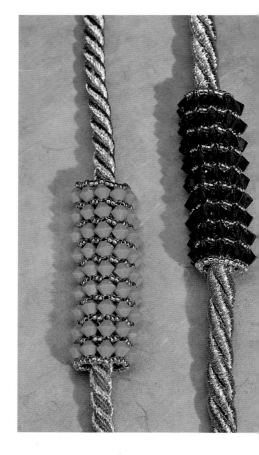

Figure 1

Figure 2

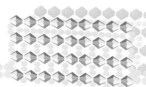

Figure 3

TO MAKE THE TASSELS

6 Cut a 1-yard (.9 m) length of beading thread, condition it, and pass it through the needle.

7 Make a strip of right-angle weave 5 units wide by 3 units long. Use the crystals to form the sides of the right-angle weave units and 2 seed beads to form the top and bottom of each unit.

8 Stitch all the first and last units together to form a long tube (as you did in step in step 4 above).

9 Weave through the beads to exit from a pair of seed beads at the top of the tube. String on 1 seed bead, pass through the next pair of seed beads, and pull snug. Continue around to form a solid ring of seed beads. Pass the needle through the first bead strung.

10 String on 33 seed beads, skip the last bead strung, and pass the needle back through the rest. Pass through the bead you just exited so your needle is going in the same direction. Repeat around the ring, working 18 simple fringe legs in all.

11 Weave through the beads to the other end of the crystal tube and repeat step 9.

12 Make the top of the tassel by using seed beads to work 1-drop tubular peyote stitch (page 18) off of the round of seed beads formed in step 6. Make sure you step up after each round.

ROUNDS 1 AND 2: Work around in tubular peyote stitch to add a total of 9 beads in each round.

Figure 4

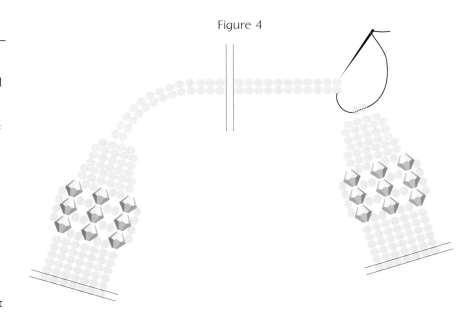

ROUNDS 3 AND 4: Make 1 decrease on each side of the round so you add a total of 7 beads.

ROUND 5: Make 1 decrease on each side of the round so you add a total of 5 beads.

ROUND 6: Work around in tubular peyote stitch, making no decreases, to add a total of 5 beads. Pass the needle through the beads added in this round and pull tight.

13 String on 2 seed beads. Pass the needle through 1 bead on the opposite side of Round 6. Weave through the beads several times to reinforce. Exit from the 2 beads just strung. Don't cut the thread. Set aside.

14 Repeat steps 6 through 13 to make another tassel.

15 Take 1 tassel and, using the working thread still attached, string on 2 seed beads. Pass the needle through the 2 beads added in step 8

and the 2 beads just strung. Repeat to make a flat, square-stitched strip 32 beads long. Check that this strip can lie across the right-angle-woven strip made in step 2 with 3 or 4 square stitches to spare on each side. Square-stitch the ladder to the 2 beads at the top of the other tassel (figure 4). Use the working thread of the other tassel to reinforce the square-stitched strip.

Cube Bead

Like a little present complete with beaded wrap, this bead is a reminder that creativity is a beautiful gift. The cube is actually six flat, peyote-stitched squares zipped together to make a box.

DESIGNED BY
Diane Fitzgerald

TECHNIQUE
Peyote stitch

FINISHED SIZE
⁷⁄₈ inch (2.2 cm)

TIPS

- If you are uncertain about where the step up will occur, count the number of A or B beads needed for each row before starting the row.

- Work with firm tension.

- Hold your work between your thumb and forefinger to keep it flat.

- Work counterclockwise if right-handed (lefties work clockwise).

- The numbers indicated at the end of each round represent the total numbers of beads added.

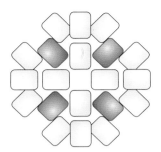

Figure 1

1 With scissors, cut a 1-yard (0.9 m) length of thread and pass it through the needle. Bring the thread ends together. Wax the thread thoroughly so the strands adhere to each other, make a knot at the end of the threads, clip the tail, and melt the ends slightly with a thread burner.

2 Make a beaded square using circular peyote stitch and the following round counts. The number of beads needed is shown in parentheses.

ROUND 1: String on 4 A beads. Slide the beads 1 inch (2.5 cm) from the knot, separate the strands between the beads and the knot, pass the needle between the strands, and pull tight so the beads form a ring. Don't let the knot to slip into a bead. Reverse direction and pass the needle back through the next bead. (4 A)

ROUND 2: String on 1 B bead and pass the needle through the next A bead from the previous round.

Repeat 3 more times and step up. These beads form the corners of the square. (4 B)

ROUND 3: String on 3 A beads and pass the needle through the next B bead. Repeat 3 more times and step up. Make sure the middle bead of the 3 beads at the corner is pushed down as shown (figure 1). (12 A)

ROUND 4: String on 2 A beads and pass the needle through the third A bead of the set of 3 at the corner. String on 1 B bead and, skipping 1 B bead in the previous round, pass the needle through the next A bead. Repeat 3 more times and step up (figure 2). (8 A, 4 B)

ROUND 5: String on 2 A beads and pass the needle into the next A bead at this corner. Work peyote stitch along the edge, using 1 B bead for each stitch. When you reach the next

Figure 2

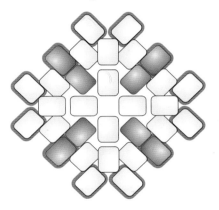

Figure 3

Figure 4　　　　　　　　　　Figure 5

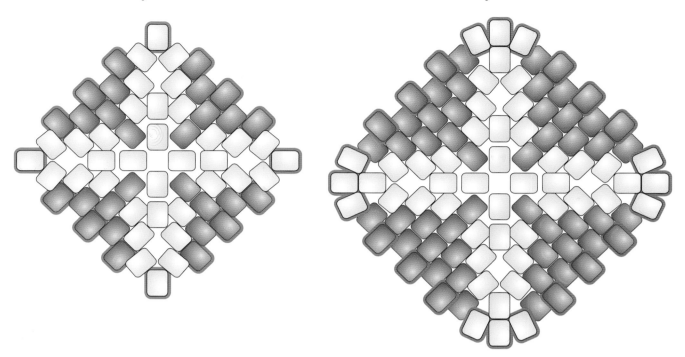

corner, repeat from the beginning of this step 3 more times and step up (figure 3). (8 A, 8 B)

ROUND 6: String on 1 A bead and pass the needle through the next A bead at this corner. Work 3 peyote stitches along the edge, using 1 B bead for each stitch. When you reach the next corner, repeat from the beginning of this step 3 more times and step up (figure 4). (4 A, 12 B)

ROUND 7: Work peyote stitch around the square using 1 B bead for each stitch. Step up. (16 B)

ROUND 8: Work 3 peyote stitches along the edge using 1 B bead for each stitch. When you reach the corner, string on 3 A beads and pass the needle through the next B bead (make sure the center bead is pushed down). Repeat from the beginning of

this step 3 more times and step up (figure 5). (12 A, 12 B)

ROUND 9: Work peyote stitch along the edges using B bead, and work the corners with 2 A beads. (16 A, 8 B)

ROUND 10: Work the corners with 1 A bead and work peyote stitch along the edges using B beads. Secure the working and tail threads and trim. Set aside.

3 Repeat steps 1 and 2 five more times so you end up with 6 squares in all.

4 Join the squares. Secure a new thread to one of the squares so it exits a corner bead. Work peyote stitch around the square using A beads. This is the base square. (24 A)

Match 1 square to each side of the base square, zipping the beads together. Secure and trim the thread.

5 Secure a new thread so it exits to the left of the upper right corner bead in the top square (see the dot marked on figure 6). Work peyote stitch using A beads along the top and left sides of the square. Exit from the bottom left corner of the square. Pass the needle into the corner bead of the base square, then into the corner bead of the square to the left and continue up the side to form the cube's first corner. Repeat to create the remaining 3 corners. You will end up with an open box shape.

6 Add the sixth side of the cube by zipping it onto the cube already formed. Secure the thread and trim.

The designer thanks Julia Pretl and her book, Little Boxes, *for the inspiration for these beads.*

132

Figure 6

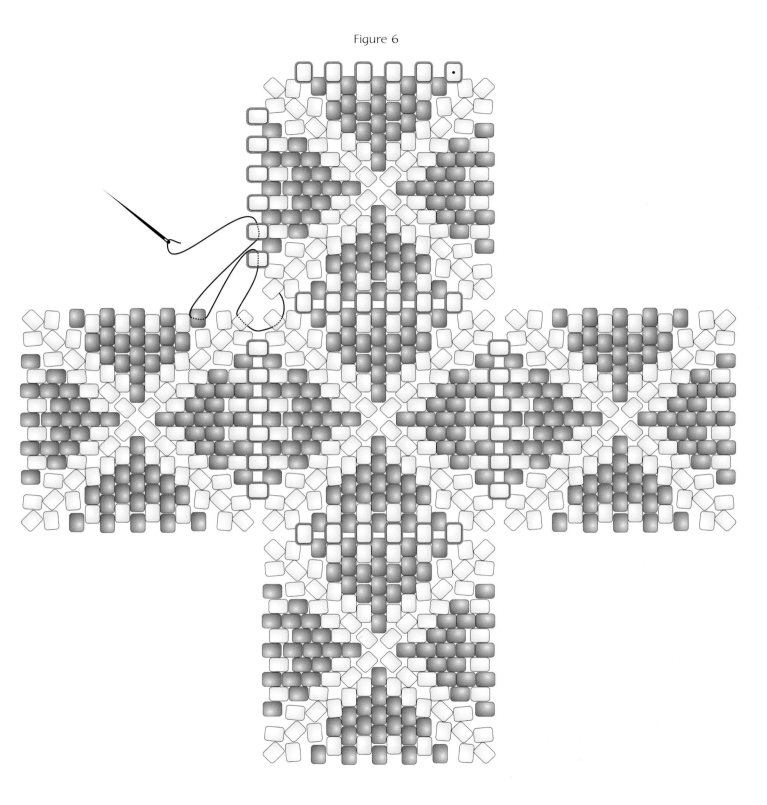

Colorful Drum Beads

These wonderful little drums of color are perfectly cylindrical—bits of beading magic. The secret is in square-stitching a beaded tube first, and then pulling it over a tiny wooden spool.

DESIGNED BY
Jan Zicarelli

TECHNIQUE
Square stitch

FINISHED SIZE
$\frac{1}{2}$ x $\frac{9}{16}$ inch
(1.3 x 1.5 cm)

MATERIALS & TOOLS

- 9 wooden spools, each $\frac{3}{8}$ x $\frac{1}{2}$ inch (9 x 13 mm)

- Black permanent marker or acrylic paint

- Scissors

- Red and green beading thread, size B

- Beeswax

- Beading needle, size 12 or 13

- Czech seed beads, size 11°, in the following colors: transparent red one-cut, transparent pink one-cut, opaque lime green one-cut, dark green-lined green, pink-lined aqua, and opaque cream

- Glue

Chart

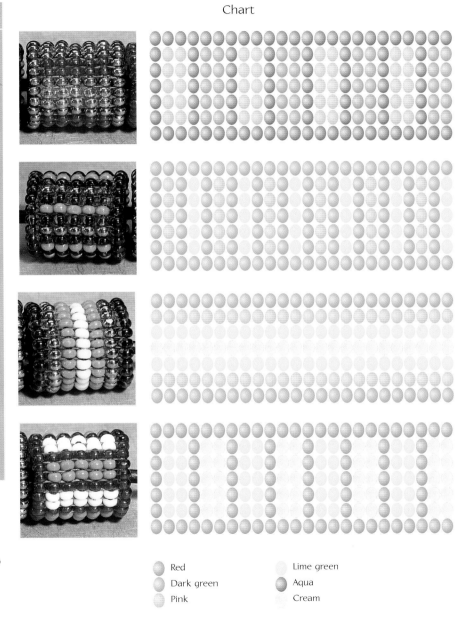

Red

Dark green

Pink

Lime green

Aqua

Cream

1 Color the ends of the spools with the marker or paint. Let the coloring dry.

2 Choose the pattern you'd like to work on, from the chart on this page or the one on the next page.

3 With the scissors, cut a 2-yard (1.8 m) length of beading thread. Use the thread color that best matches

Chart

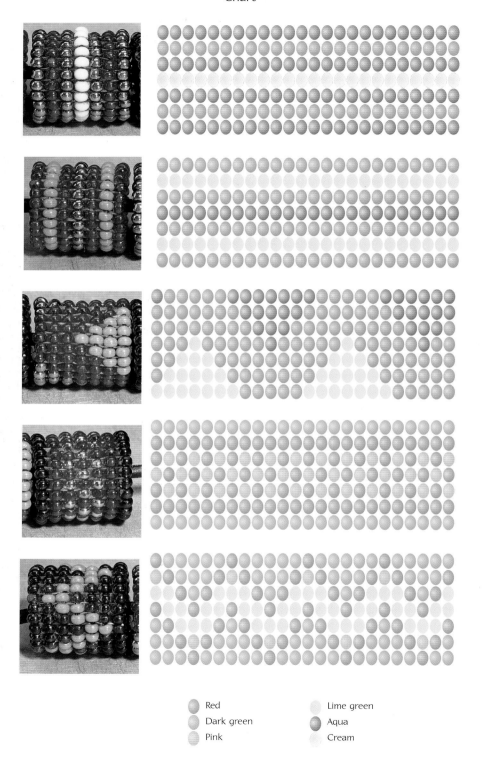

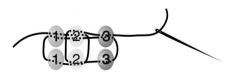

- ● Red
- ● Dark green
- ● Pink
- ● Lime green
- ● Aqua
- ● Cream

the beads in the chart you chose. Wax the thread and pass it through the needle.

4 Make the base circle. Begin by stringing on Beads 1 and 2 of the first row and Beads 2 and 1 of the second row. Slide them 8 inches (20.5 cm) from the end of the thread. Pass the needle through Beads 1 and 2 of the first row again.

String on Bead 3 of the first row and Bead 3 of the second row. Pass the needle through Bead 2 of the second row and Beads 2 and 3 of the first row (figure 1). Repeat this step, adding the next bead of both the first and the second rows until you have 24 beads in each row.

Bend the strip so the first and last beads of each row touch. Square-stitch the beads together to make a circle.

5 Work the rest of the pattern in tubular square stitch.

6 Once Round 7 is completed, slide the beaded bead onto the painted spool and pass the needle

Figure 1

through all the beads of Round 7 again, pulling tightly so the beaded bead fits snugly on the end of the spool. Secure the working thread and trim.

7 Thread the tail through the needle. Pass the needle through all the beads of Round 1, pulling tightly so the beaded bead fits snugly on this end of the spool. Secure the thread and trim.

8 If the finished bead is a little loose on the spool, apply a small amount of glue to the outer rim at each end of the spool.

TIPS

- Not all size 11° seed beads are the same size. The Czech seed beads used in the beaded beads shown measure 18 beads per inch (2.5 cm). If bigger or smaller beads are used, the finished bead will not fit on the spool properly.

- Depending on the beads, it may be necessary to use a size 13 beading needle, especially when going back through all the beads in a row and when burying the thread ends.

- Be selective when you choose which bead to put on your needle. Variances in bead sizes will show.

Gallery

JoAnn Baumann
Elemental, 2004
45.7 cm long (necklace)
Seed beads, pressed glass beads; Ndebele stitch
Photo © Larry Sanders

Twirly Bead

Envision a twirling barbershop pole dipped in candy, and you have this bead. The seemingly complicated pattern is actually easy to create using tubular peyote stitch—the spiral unfolds as you change bead sizes in each stitch.

DESIGNED BY
Kathy Seely

TECHNIQUE
Peyote stitch

FINISHED SIZE
$^7/_{16}$ x 2$^1/_2$ inches
(1.4 x 6.3 cm)

MATERIALS & TOOLS

- Scissors
- Beading thread, size D
- Beading needle, size 10
- Japanese seed beads in color A, size 11°
- Round Japanese seed beads in color B, size 8°
- Triangular Japanese seed beads in color C, size 8°
- Japanese cylinder beads in color D
- Beading form (knitting needle, crochet hook, or wooden skewer)
- Masking tape (optional)
- Permanent markers in color to match size 11° beads (optional)

1   With the scissors, cut a 1½-yard (1.4 m) length of thread and pass it through the needle. String on 1 A bead and turn it into a stop bead. Place the bead about 3 inches (7.5 cm) from the end of the thread. The stop bead will be incorporated into the beaded bead.

2   String on 1 A, 2 B, 2 C, 2 B, 2 A, and 4 D. Pass the needle through the stop bead and pull tight to create a base circle. Pass the needle through all the beads again and exit from the second B bead strung.

3   Slide the circle onto the beading form. Make sure the circle fits snugly on the form. If the beads are too loose, wrap a section of the form (about ¾ inch [1.9 cm] around) with several thicknesses of tape until the circle fits well. You will be able to remove the form when the beadwork is long enough to handle, after 5 rounds or so.

4   Work rounds of tubular peyote stitch. (The beads in the circle make up Rounds 1 and 2.)

ROUNDS 3–59: Using firm thread tension (page 13), work each stitch in this order: 1 B, 1 C, 1 B, 1 A, 1 D, 1 D, and 1 A. Make a step up by passing the needle through the bead you first exited and the first bead added in this round. (You will step up after each round.)

Note: To help keep track of your bead placement, remember that the bead you string on to stitch is the same type of bead your thread is exiting.

5   Secure the tail and working threads and trim. If the exposed thread on the stop bead is too noticeable, color it with a marker.

Designer Profiles

SHARON BATEMAN is a mixed-media artist, best known for her many magazine articles, appearances on DIY's Jewelry Making show, and beading books that include *Findings and Finishings* (Interweave Press, 2003) and her self-published titles *Morning Rose Rosette* (2001), *Peepers and Creepers* (2000), and *Over the Edge* (2005). She invented and manufactures Sharondipity Tube Looms, which are clear plastic looms designed for specific projects. She is available for questions or comments at www.sharonbateman.com.

JOANN BAUMANN is a seasoned bead artist who specializes in complex sculptural creations, most recently self-supporting structures and floral designs. Her beadwork has been featured in many publications, the latest being *The Art of Beadwork* (Watson-Guptill, 2005). She has taught all over the United States, including at the *Bead & Button* Show in Milwaukee, Wisconsin. Her work continues to be exhibited nationally. She lives in Glencoe, Illinois, and can be reached at joann@jdesigns.org.

INGRID GOLDBLOOM BLOCH is a mixed-media sculptor who sees beauty in everyday objects. Her works have been featured in museums and galleries throughout the United States, including two Bead International Best in Contemporary Beadwork touring shows and the SOHO20 Gallery in New York. Ingrid's work has appeared in *500 Beaded Objects* (Lark Books, 2004), and in several magazines, such as *Fiberarts, Surface Design Journal, Bead & Button,* and *Beadwork.* Ingrid lives in Massachusetts and can be reached at igoldblo@wheatonma.edu.

TINA BLOOMENTHAL enjoys working with all sizes and shapes of beads, and creating jewelry and sculptural objects is a passion. She loves to create new color palettes and experiment with forms and textures. Contact Tina at tzbloom@aol.com.

MARCIA LAGING CUMMINGS has been working with seed beads for 10 years. Inspired by a Joyce Scott necklace she owns, she subsequently took a workshop from Joyce and has been beading ever since. Her work has been featured in *Beadwork* magazine, at three *Bead & Button* Shows, at the Dairy Barn's Best in Contemporary Beadwork (2002, 2004, 2006), and in *500 Beaded Objects* (Lark Books, 2004).

MARSHA DAVIS has been teaching beading and seed beadwork for more than 10 years. Since 2000 she has been on the faculty at the 92nd Street Y School of the Arts' jewelry and metalsmithing department, and she also teaches workshops in the New York City area for the American Museum of Natural History, Beads by Blanche, and the Bead Society of Greater New York, as well as at the new Sugar Maples Center for Arts and Education in upstate New York. Contact Marsha at marimda@verizon.net.

REV. WENDY ELLSWORTH is a celebrated beadwork artist and teacher whose work has been published extensively in beading books and magazines. Her work has also been featured in many exhibition venues, including Connecticut's Brookfield Craft Center, SOFA NY, the Dairy Barn in Athens, Ohio, and the Los Angeles Craft and Folk Museum. Wendy is inspired by the colors of nature and currently works in a free-form beading style, depending only on spontaneity and improvisation. Contact Wendy at wendy@ellsworthstudios.com.

DIANE FITZGERALD is the author of eight beadwork books and has taught beadwork since 1989. She is an avid glass bead collector. You may contact her through her website: www.dianefitzgerald.com.

RUTH ANN GRIM is an active beadwork artist who has taught across the East Coast. She has had several of her works published in *Beadwork* magazine and is the communications coordinator of the Bead Society of

Eastern Pennsylvania. Ruth lives in Sellersville, Pennsylvania, where she can be contacted at ruthannbeads@msn.com.

CAROLE HORN is a native New Yorker who worked in a variety of media before becoming fascinated with beads. She doesn't begin with a finished beading project in mind, but experiments with technique and color until something wonderful unfolds and surprises her.

GILLIAN LAMB is a seasoned knitter who fell in love with beading in 1998 after working with patterning software. She has taught extensively in the United Kingdom and the United States, and her work has been published in many books. Gillian has been very active in the Beadworker's Guild (U.K.) and, in 2001, earned the top prize for the guild's annual challenge. Gillian lives in Surrey, England, and can be reached at http://www.gillianlamb.co.uk/.

D. JEKA LAMBERT has a background in interior and theatrical costume design. She teaches beadwork at bead stores and through adult education programs in the San Francisco Bay area and has been creating beaded jewelry since 1999. Jeka's work can be seen at the Valley Art Gallery in Walnut Creek, California.

YOSHIE MARUBASHI was born in Ginza Tokyo, Japan. She worked as a professional jeweler and wax model maker for a major New York City jewelry company and has 25 years' experience as a professional beadworker and teacher. Yoshie was profiled in a feature article in the October/November 2003 issue of *Beadwork* magazine. Contact Yoshie at yoshiem@att.net or www.yoshiesjewel.com.

MARISSA MCCONNELL lives in Plymouth, Minnesota, where she owns a shop named Insomniac Beads. She has been beading for as long as she can remember and is still learning something new every day.

ALYSE MIDDLETON is a multidiscipline crafter with a focus on functional art, especially fiber arts. With her mother, JoAnn Baumann, Alyse has taught classes at the *Bead & Button* Show and the North Shore NeedleArts Guild. Alyse lives and works in northern Illinois.

PAULA PARMENTER is a beadworker who specializes in off-loom Russian stitches and dream catchers. She has taught classes extensively throughout the United States, including the 2004 and 2005 *Bead & Button* Shows. Paula's work has been published in *500 Beaded Objects*

(Lark Books, 2004) and has been featured in prominent bead suppliers' advertisements. Paula lives in Phoenix, Arizona, with her husband, daughter, and a "family zoo." She can be contacted at bead@teacher.com.

CHRISTINE PRUSSING is a beadwork designer and teacher. Her work has been widely published in beading magazines and books, and she is the author of *Beading with Right-Angle Weave* (Interweave Press, 2004). Christine owns The Bead Gallery in Juneau, Alaska, where she has lived for almost 30 years.

ELFLEDA RUSSELL explores in beading the same figurative and natural themes that underlie her painting. Through the opulent, tactile medium of beading, she discovers more fanciful expressions of these themes. Textile methods are sometimes incorporated. Elfleda has been honored with several international beading and textile design awards, has exhibited internationally in many media, and has had many beaded works published. She enjoys teaching and is the author of numerous articles and the book *Off-Loom Weaving* (Little Brown, 1975).

Designer Profiles *(continued)*

KATHY SEELY was influenced early on by her seamstress grandmother, who had a keen sense of detail and a fondness for playing with color and thread. Beads fit Kathy's artistic temperament perfectly, and she has been beading since 1992. Her work has been shown in galleries and museums throughout the United States and is in several public and private collections. Kathy is the owner of Moonbead Beads and Beadwork in Oak Ridge, Tennessee, where she teaches regularly.

MARY TAFOYA is a beadworker who mixes advanced bead-embroidery techniques with various other media to create memorable pieces about women, spirituality, and mythology. She is a frequent contributor to *Beadwork* magazine and teaches in Albuquerque, New Mexico, as well as other venues. Mary was raised in Louisville, Kentucky, and now resides with her family in Albuquerque, New Mexico, where she launched and maintains Aunt Molly's Bead Street, an online educational resource for beadworkers. Contact Mary at http://home.flash.net/ ~mjtafoya/mary/contact.htm.

JOANNE WATERS has been beading and teaching beading for about 10 years. She had a write-up on beaded frogs in the June/July 2001 *Bead & Button* magazine. Her beaded frogs were also featured in a book, *Beaded*

Critters (Kalmbach Publishing, 2004). She lives in West Vancouver, British Columbia, where she also works in therapeutic recreation with seniors.

NANCY ZELLERS enjoys designing beadwork projects that are deceptively minimalist yet challenging to execute. She teaches internationally, exhibits in contemporary art shows, and publishes in beadwork magazines and books. Contact Nancy at nzbeads@aol.com.

JAN ZICARELLI is a beadwork artist and teacher who specializes in sculptural techniques. Her work has been shown in many national exhibits and has been published in *Myths & Folktales* (Caravan Beads, 2000), *500 Beaded Objects* (Lark Books, 2004), *Bead Dreams* (Bead & Button, 2005), *500 Baskets* (Lark Books, 2006), *Beadwork* magazine, and *Bead & Button* magazine. Jan lives in Excelsior, Minnesota, with her husband and two teenage sons and enjoys spending the winters in Tucson, Arizona.

Index

Beads, 9–10

Daisy chain, 46

Decreases, defined, 14

Down beads, 16

Embellishments, 21

Fringe, 21

Herringbone stitch, 15
  Projects using, 27, 54, 67, 75, 90, 114

Increases, defined, 14

Knots, 13

Ladder stitch, 14–15
  Projects using, 27, 54, 67, 75

Needles, beading, 11–12

Netting, 15
  Projects using, 64, 93, 118, 124

Peyote stitch, 15–18
  Projects using, 24, 33, 38, 44, 50, 52,
  60, 64–83, 87, 90, 96, 100, 106, 112,
  121, 127, 130, 138

Picots, 21

Reinforcing, 12

Right-angle weave, 19–20
  Projects using, 30, 41, 46, 70, 102,
  106, 109, 127

Rounds, defined, 12

Rows, defined, 12

Square stitch, 18–19
  Projects using, 22, 24, 33, 46, 57,
  127, 134

Step ups, defined 14

Stitch in the ditch, 21

Stop beads, 13–14

Techniques, stitching, 14–21

Tension, 13

Thread, 11

Thread-related terms, 13–14

Tools, 11–12

Triangle weave, 41

Up beads, 16

Zipping up, 16